The Quiet Revolution of Pope Francis

A Synodal Catholic Church in Ireland?

'No! New wine, fresh skins!' (Mk 2: 22)

Gerry O'Hanlon SJ

First published in 2018 by Messenger Publications

ISBN 978 1 78812 000 5

Page 39 quotation from Seamus Heaney, 'Out of this World', in *District and Circle*,
London: Faber & Faber, 2006. Reproduced with kind permission.
Cover Photograph: Giulio Napolitano / Shutterstock

Designed by Messenger Publications Design Department
Typeset in Times New Roman & Albertina
Printed by Johnswood Press Ltd

Messenger Publications,
37 Lower Leeson Street, Dublin D02 W938
www.messenger.ie

CONTENTS

Abbreviations

LG: *Lumen Gentium*, Dogmatic Constitution on the Church,
21 November 1964

GS: *Gaudium et Spes*, Constitution on the Church in the
Modern World, 7 December 1965

DH: *Dignitatis Humanae*, Declaration on Religious Freedom,
7 December 1965

UR: *Unitatis Redintegratio*, Decree on Ecumenism,
21 November 1964 Interview: A Big Heart Open to
God, Interview with Pope Francis to Jesuit journals,
19 September 2013

EG: *Evangelii Gaudium*, Apostolic Exhortation of Pope Francis,
The Joy of the Gospel, 24 November 2013

LS: *Laudato Si'*, Encyclical Letter of Pope Francis, Praised Be,
On Care for our Common Home, 24 May 2015

Address: Pope Francis' Address at Commemorative
Ceremony for the Fiftieth Anniversary of the Synod
of Bishops, 17 October 2015

AL: *Amoris Laetitia*, Apostolic Exhortation of Pope Francis,
The Joy of Love, 19 March 2016

GE: *Gaudete et Exsultate*, Apostolic Exhortation of Pope
Francis, Rejoice and Be Glad, On the Call to Holiness
in Today's World, 19 March 2018 (released on 9 April 2018)

SF: *Sensus Fidei* in the Life of the Church, International
Theological Commission, 10 June 2014

TT: Theology Today, International Theological Commission,
8 March 2012

Sp. Ex.:   Spiritual Exercises of St Ignatius

OS: *Ordinatio Sacerdotalis*, Apostolic Letter of Pope John Paul II,
22 May 1994

DV: *Dei Verbum*, Dogmatic Constitution on Divine Revelation,
18 November 1965

InterIn: *Inter Insigniores*, Declaration on the Question of Admission
of Women to the Ministerial Priesthood, 15 October 1976.
UUS: *Ut Unum Sint*, Encyclical Letter of Pope John II,
25 May 1995.

FOREWORD

It is well known that Pope Francis is trying to reform the Catholic Church. At the 2013 conclave that elected him, he was given an explicit mandate to renew the Church *ad intra* and *ad extra*. To that end he has held a number of important synods in Rome on evangelisation, the family and marriage, and an upcoming synod on youth in October 2018. In addition he has published a series of visionary documents: *The Joy of the Gospel* [EG] (2013), which is programmatic for renewal, *On Care for our Common Home* [LS] (2015) addressed to all people on the planet, *The Joy of Love* [AL] (2016), which is focused on marriage and love in family, and *Rejoice and Be Glad* [GE] (2018), which is subtitled *A Call to Holiness in Today's World.*

However, the question arises: Is anybody listening, is anything happening on the ground, are there any signs of change taking place in the Church? One person who has been listening and making things happen on the ground and effecting change is Gerry O' Hanlon SJ.

O'Hanlon is a Jesuit priest, a highly respected theologian and a former provincial of the Irish Jesuits. As a Jesuit he is well placed to understand the mind of the first Jesuit pope. As a theologian he knows better than most how to scrutinise the signs of the times and interpret them in the light of the gospel. As a former provincial of the Irish Jesuits he is aware that leadership involves processes of consultation, communal discernment and decision-making in the service of the mission of Christ in the world and the coming Reign of God.

The publication of *The Quiet Revolution of Pope Francis – A Synodal Catholic Church in Ireland?* offers a new programme of renewal for the Catholic Church in Ireland. This program is rooted in the Bible, Tradition, the Second Vatican Council and the teaching of Pope Francis.

It is often said that all politics is local and equally it can be said that the experience of Church is local. In this new book O'Hanlon offers an Irish theology for a Church in crisis, carefully crafted in the light of his experience of having travelled the length and breadth of Ireland over the last ten years in response to invitations to speak at gatherings of parishes, of priests and of individual bishops.

This is not an armchair theology but one that has been chiselled out of the experience of listening to and learning from others in high and low places, engaging with diverse groups, attending to the teaching of the Second Vatican Council, and heeding the prophetic voice of the bishop of Rome.

The book is timely: it addresses the challenges facing the life of the Church in a secularised culture, it coincides with the visit of Pope Francis to Ireland in late August 2018 for the world meeting of families and it outlines how parishes and dioceses can implement the teaching of the Second Vatican Council and the synodal vision of Pope Francis.

O'Hanlon is clear that a reform of the Church requires the following steps: a renewed encounter with the living Christ, a recovery of the missionary mandate of Christ, a reading of the signs of the times, a listening to the 'sense of the faith' among all the people of God, an engagement with other theologians, attention to the teaching of bishops and a communal discernment of the promptings of the Holy Spirit – all with a view to implementing the practice of synodality as presented by the vision and praxis of Pope Francis. The recovery of the principle of synodality is offered as the way forward in the renewing of parishes, of dioceses, of national conferences of bishops and of the universal Church. A synodal model of Church offers a different way of being Church, more in tune with the demands of the twenty-first century. Synodality is the red thread woven through the nine chapters.

O'Hanlon does not duck the hard questions like the role of women in ministry and Church, the exercise of power and authority, the participation of the baptised in the one priesthood of Christ, the institutional resistance to change and the importance of respect for conscience. Nor does he have any illusions about the cultural challenges surrounding any reform of the Church in a post-Christian society. These include the relegation of religion to the private sphere, the presence of an individualism that is indifferent to the common good, the denial of transcendence and the emergence of relativity as the flavour of the day and a market-driven capitalism that all too often results in exclusion.

A striking feature of this book is its balance, its even-handedness, and its respect for other points of view. O'Hanlon represents both sides of the debate and then moves forward into a higher synthesis. The book is constructively critical of the ecclesial status quo, and yet it is full of hope for the future.

This book, coming at this time, is a gift to the Catholic Church: it seeks to inform decision-making processes in planning for the future, it establishes a recovery of the Second Vatican Council's principle of mutuality that should exist between the Church and the world, it outlines the underlying principles of synodality and the challenges that a synodal model of Church entails. These challenges demand a respect for the fundamental equality of the baptised, an honest sharing of faith and doubt, an outreach to the alienated, an openness to the searching questions of others and the faithful, the promotion of new forms of shared participation in governance at parish and diocesan levels and a renewed commitment to the mission of Christ.

In my opinion, this book is a prophetic text, a landmark study offering a way forward for the Church in Ireland, and a roadmap for the reform of the Church. It will be of value to all the members of the Church: theff People of God, women and men in ministry, parish pastoral councils, priests and religious, theologians and bishops.

I recommend this book enthusiastically to all who care about the future of the Catholic Church in Ireland and to all who have walked away, for a variety of reasons, from the Church. May all hear the call to reform in *The Quiet Revolution of Pope Francis – A Synodal Catholic Church in Ireland?* as a wake-up call for a slumbering Church.

Dermot A. Lane
Balally Parish
April 2018

INTRODUCTION

I dream of a 'missionary option', that is, a missionary impulse capable of transforming everything, so that the Church's customs, ways of doing things, times and schedules, language and structures can be suitably channelled for the evangelisation of today's world rather than for her self-preservation. (EG, 27)

Pope Francis begins his Apostolic Exhortation *Evangelii Gaudium* (2013) with the upbeat proclamation that the '… Joy of the Gospel fill the hearts of all those who encounter Jesus' (EG, 1).

However, it is well known that when Francis was elected bishop of Rome and pope earlier that year in 2013, it was at a time of little joy for the Catholic Church. In the meetings of cardinals leading up to his election many grave problems were mentioned: the scandal of child sexual abuse, suspected financial and other improprieties within the Vatican itself, the ongoing contested reception of the Second Vatican Council, the many economic and social injustices experienced by the marginalised worldwide, the role of women in the Church, disputes about teaching on sexual morality, the shortage of priests in many parts of the world, to name but some of the many difficult issues. The atmosphere was troubled. There was a sense that the Church had lost its way, was no longer a sacrament or sign for the world of Jesus Christ and his Kingdom, a sign of hope. Instead, despite the ongoing wonderful witness of so many, it seemed like almost an anti-sign, an easy target for unsympathetic enemies and unconvincing even to many of its friends.

Ireland has not escaped this sense of crisis. There has been a huge loss of moral authority due to the mishandling of the clerical child sexual abuse scandal. In addition, for various reasons, the Church found itself ill-prepared to face the growing challenges of secularisation, modernity and post-modernity. There was particular focus on the role of the Church in civil society in areas like health and education, not to mention in debates about same-sex marriage and abortion. There was, in addition, growing awareness of the shortage of priests, the silencing of some prominent clerical voices, and the neuralgic issue around how women are treated in the Church. There continues to be the ongoing haemorrhaging of young people from the Church, a sense that there is a disconnect, a lack of that 'Velcro-effect' that might attach the language of faith to the lived experience of life.

What became clear from the very first moments of the pontificate of Francis was that he seemed to sense the depths of the problem. It has become apparent since that he has a clear and radical strategic response. This book will explore the nature of the problem in a little more detail (Part One: Setting the Scene), and then analyse the response of Francis in its main aspects (Part Two: Pope Francis and the Quiet Revolution) and the issues which arise (Part Three: Emerging Issues). It will conclude with a reflection on how we in Ireland can best respond in a critically constructive way to his proposals (Part Four: Ireland Revisited). I have rehearsed much of this analysis in previously published articles, all of which are referred to in the bibliography.

Francis, I will suggest, has made two very significant contributions to our understanding of Church reform. Firstly, he has located the issues of renewal and reform within the more basic truth of our encounter with Jesus Christ and the missionary impulse this generates – including the joy of discipleship and the outreach to the peripheries and to the marginalised ('a poor Church for the poor'). This outward-looking location means that reform is not simply self-referential, better organisational structures for their own sake: no, reform always functions with respect to mission. In principle at least this missionary focus can help to unite a Church which had become weary of fruitless battles between liberals and conservatives.

Secondly, and crucially, Francis has identified the institutional and cultural shape of the reform he envisages: the Church for the third millennium must be synodal, collegial, an 'inverted pyramid', in which the People of God are primary and the hierarchy in all its forms are there to serve the People in whom the Holy Spirit is present. Francis believes that this kind of model of Church is more suitable for our age, while being rooted in Scripture and tradition. He is well aware that liberals and conservatives will continue to disagree on many important issues, but he believes that a synodal Church, which learns how to discern communally, is more able to live through these conflicts in a way that is fruitful and not demoralising. And, more importantly for this missionary-focused bishop of Rome, he believes that a synodal Church is a more appropriate institutional and cultural place from which to dialogue with our world, which, often without realising it, has great need of the hope and good news which comes from the gospel of Jesus Christ.

This crucial focus on a synodal way of being Church has been spoken about by Francis himself as not just an era of change, but 'a change of era'.[1] It is a paradigm shift, a fundamental change which goes beyond even important adjustments to the existing model of Church. We are speaking here of a revolution, in the sense of a radical change to an existing structure. This change is, however, non-violent, and it recalls an original cosmological and astronomical meaning of the term revolution (to turn back; revolving around a centre), in that the fundamental change is also a return to a previous way of being Church, albeit now with appropriate adjustments for changed times. This quiet, velvet revolution can easily be missed by other striking features of this papacy and by the failure of the rest of us – including hierarchies – to appreciate what is at stake. It is my hope that this book may contribute to raising awareness of what is involved, to teasing out what Francis is proposing, and assessing its suitability, with particular reference to Ireland.

Of course there is no guarantee that Francis will be successful in what he is trying to achieve. There is much opposition, and a great deal of apathy. He is in the ironic position of having the appearance to the world of a celebrity-monarch trying to abolish monarchy and celebrity. He is, instead, trying to encourage a more adult, participatory institutional model, with a leadership of service. It

1 Address by Pope Francis to Italian bishops in Florence, 10 November 2015 – see *The Tablet*, 11 November 2015.

would be easy – and a papal visit offers the ideal but fatal temptation in this direction – to surf the wave of the papal popularity of Francis, or to applaud some particular areas of reform and still miss the wood for the trees: Francis is proposing something more strategic, more revolutionary and more durable. Along with this model of Church comes the promise of a new capacity to resolve over time the many single issues of contention which now appear intractable. It will require imagination and critical engagement from other agents in the Church if the change he envisages is to happen.

PART ONE

Setting the Scene:
Nazareth, Rome and Ireland

CHAPTER ONE

Background to the Crisis: the Roman Catholic Church

Our aim is to search for better balances without damaging vital forces. (Ladislas Orsy, *Receiving the Council*, 2009)

There were seven pre-conclave assemblies, known as general congregations, in the lead-up to the election of Pope Francis in 2013. In these assemblies it became clear that the Church's maladroit handling of the scandal of clerical child sexual abuse was one of the issues uppermost in the mind of the cardinals. However, '… that was only part of what was seen as a dysfunctional Vatican bureaucracy in which various Curia departments were operating in an autonomous and high-handed manner, issuing instructions to bishops around the world with the authority of the Pope but without his knowledge'.[2] There was evidence of financial and sexual impropriety. There was a sense of crisis, and again and again there were calls for reform, and, in particular, a return to a more collegial Church.[3]

Up to the Second Vatican Council
Ecclesiologists commonly note that the New Testament evidence is relatively non-prescriptive about what counts as normative for the Church in terms of institution and structures.[4] Discipleship, mission,

---

2 Paul Vallely, *Pope Francis, Untying the Knots*, London: Bloomsbury, 2013, 151–2.
3 See Vallely, op. cit., chapters 7 and 8; Austen Ivereigh, *The Great Reformer, Francis and the Making of a Radical Pope*, London: Allen & Unwin, 2014, chapter 9; Marco Politi, *Pope Francis Among the Wolves, The Inside Story of a Revolution*, New York: Columbia University Press, 2015 (second edition), chapter 4.
4 For what follows, see Gerry O'Hanlon, *A New Vision for the Catholic Church: A View from Ireland*, Dublin: Columba Press, 2011, and Richard McBrien, *The Church*, New York: Harper Collins, 2009.

Eucharist, the promise of the ongoing presence of the Holy Spirit, the distinct identity of the Twelve with a certain pre-eminence of Peter within the group – all this is entirely compatible with a plurality of ecclesial structures. So, for example, ecclesiologist Michael Fahy, drawing on Raymond Brown, notes the diversity of churches and structures that existed in early Christianity, and identifies over ten such different types and structures. These are modelled after the different theological outlooks of the likes of Matthew, Paul and John, with both women and men playing prominent and diverse roles, and with local Churches experiencing the freedom to develop their own style of organisation in response to particular situation and needs.

It is notable that during that period there also existed a dynamic interplay between what we would now call collegial and primatial principles of authority – *the* burning and deeply conflictual issue of the early Church, the mission to and identity of the Gentiles, was resolved over time through the Council of Jerusalem and with key interventions from Paul and a somewhat chastened Peter (see Gal 2:11).

Over time, as the Church grew in numbers and spread geographically, a greater uniformity of structure did develop properly. Not that everything about this new uniformity was necessarily helpful or from the Holy Spirit – one thinks, for example, of the post-Constantinian quasi-identification of Church and state in which '... the clergy became, in effect, civil servants with all of the advantages, financial and otherwise, attached thereto'.[5] Titles, honour, dress – they all date from this period and are early pointers to the ever-present temptation towards clericalism.

For the best part of the first millennium it seems that, despite growing institutionalisation and the increasing prestige of the bishop of Rome, a synodal, collegial culture flourished, at different levels – local, regional and universal (ecumenical councils). This historical reality reminds us that, apart from the relatively few normative elements from the New Testament, and those limited historical developments which have attained normative status, the

5   McBrien, ibid., 66.

Church remains free to adjust her culture and structures to best carry out the mission which has been given her – in other words, in the light of the particular situation and pastoral needs of succeeding generations and cultures. In this context the words of Michael Fahy about the Church in the second and third centuries are instructive: 'What needs to be explained about the early church is not how a local, city-based church came to see itself as autonomous, but rather how a local church came to choose various modalities for wider fellowship. For mainline Christian churches, being autonomous never meant sterile isolation'.[6] The default position, in other words, was autonomy in communion.

A shift occurred with the Gregorian Reform of the eleventh century (Pope Gregory VII, 1073–85). Often, again for very good reasons (think, for example, of the need to free the Church from political domination of various forms over the centuries, beginning with Gregory himself in his relationship with the German Emperor Henry IV), the Church became more centralised and monarchical. This trend reached its apogee in the nineteenth century with the First Vatican Council in 1870 and its definitions of papal primacy and infallibility.

Historian John O'Malley speaks of this whole period (from the French Revolution of 1789 up to the election of John XXIII as pope in 1958) as the 'Long Nineteenth Century'.[7] It is characterised not just by an entirely new 'papalisation' of the Catholic Church (a move from considering the Petrine office very much along the lines of 'first among equals', a court of last appeal, to a much more hands-on assumption of absolute, monarchical power, aided by the Roman Curia). There is also, with the exception of the emergence of Catholic social teaching in Leo XIII's 1891 *Rerum Novarum*, a turn inwards by the Church away from a world which it mistrusts and sees as hostile. Bruised by the violent anti-clericalism of the French Revolution, the Church of this period rejects that cluster of developments arising from the Enlightenment, capitalism, the

---

6 O'Hanlon, op. cit., 20.
7 See John W. O'Malley, *What Happened at Vatican II,* Harvard, Mass: Harvard University Press, 2008, chapter 2: see also Gerry O'Hanlon, op. cit., chapter 2, and McBrien, op. cit., Parts III and IV, 85–149.

Industrial Revolution and democracy, which came to be known as Modernism or Liberalism. This new culture treasured the rights and freedom of the individual, and Protestantism, with its focus on the individual conscience, was more attuned to its development.

And so, despite the careful qualifiers to be found in the decrees of the First Vatican Council with respect to papal primacy and infallibility, the popular imagination and the effective operational culture of the Catholic Church assumed an unmitigated centralist, ultramontanist hue.[8] The phrase 'creeping infallibility', attributed to Yves Congar, also extended to primacy so that, in the words of O'Malley, '... as a consequence, Catholics looked increasingly to "Rome" not only as a court of final appeal but for answers to all questions'.[9]

All this was accompanied by the relegation of laity to a very secondary role in the Church, much in contrast to New Testament and early Church times. In his Encyclical against Modernism (*Pascendi*, 1907) Pius X referred to '... that most pernicious doctrine which would make of the laity a factor of progress in the church' and condemned Modernist positions which held that '... ecclesiastical government requires reformation in all its branches ... [that] a share in ecclesiastical government should therefore be given to the lower ranks of the clergy and even to the laity, and authority should be decentralised ... [that] the Roman Congregations, especially the Congregations of the Index and the Holy Office, are to be reformed'.[10] The same pope, in an encyclical to the French Church a year earlier (*Vehementer,* 1906), reiterated the hierarchical structure of the Church, '... the Church is essentially an unequal society comprising two categories of persons, the Pastors and the flock, those who occupy a rank in the different degrees of the hierarchy and the multitude of the faithful. So distinct are these two categories that with the pastoral body only rests the necessary right and authority for promoting the end of the society and directing all its members towards that end; the one duty of the multitude is to

8   Gerry O'Hanlon, op. cit. 25.
9   O'Malley, op. cit., 56.
10 John W. O'Malley, op. cit., 69–70.

allow themselves to be led, and, like a docile flock, to follow the Pastors'.[11] The contrast with the teachings of the Second Vatican Council and Pope Francis is stark.

This is some of the background to the Second Vatican Council. There were significant exceptions to the analysis presented here – the Holy Spirit can never be entirely stifled and breaches of this rather uniform and repressive scenario were frequent, not least in the genuine piety and works of charity, mercy and justice of so many individuals and groups. One also thinks in this respect of the period between the First and Second Vatican Councils when Catholic scripture and liturgical scholarship began to flourish, when neo-Thomism became more outward looking and began to engage with secular scholarship, when the *nouvelle théologie* movement initiated that *ressourcement* movement, returning beyond Thomas and the Medievalists to patristic and biblical sources for theological nourishment. There was, in addition, as already mentioned, the emergence of that engaged corpus of Catholic social teaching, and, not least in Ireland, with Frank Duff and his Legionaries of Mary, the emergence of different lay groups which challenged the centralist assumption of lay inferiority. And, of course, there was enormous strength in the tightly knit administrative structure that enabled Rome to watch over local Churches and allowed Catholics worldwide to experience a strong sense of identity and belonging.

Despite these positive signs, it became evident, at least in retrospect, that all was not well with the Church in the lead-up to the Second Vatican Council. Canonist and theologian Ladislas Orsy speaks about the ongoing aim '… to search for better balances without damaging vital forces'.[12] And Pope Pius XI captures this well in remarks made in 1939, just before his own death, to a group of young Canadian seminarians who were completing their studies in Rome: 'I want you to take this message away with you. The Church, the Mystical Body of Christ, has become a monstrosity. The head is very large, but the body is shrunken. You, the priests,

---

11 Ibid., 25.
12 Ladislas Orsy, *Receiving the Council, Theological and Canonical Insights and Debates*, Collegeville, MN: Liturgical Press, 2009, 12.

must rebuild the body of the Church and the only way that you can rebuild it is to mobilise the lay people.'[13]

The Second Vatican Council (1962–65)[14]

The Second Vatican Council reversed the two dominant trends that we have identified as being characteristic of the culture and structure of the Catholic Church over the 'long nineteenth century' and before – it displayed an openness to the world and to dialogue with it, and it proposed a collegial rather than a monarchical vision of Church.

This unforeseen outcome was, however, very much in the spirit of Pope John XXIII's opening address in which he distanced himself from a hostile, condemnatory attitude towards the world and recommended instead the 'medicine of mercy rather than of severity'.[15] The idiom or style of the council was pastoral in an unprecedented way – persuasion rather than legal declaration was its mode of proceeding. This was not, however, a pastoral approach divorced from doctrine or even dogma – rather, as the Dogmatic Constitution on Divine Revelation makes so clear, truth in scriptural terms is always 'saving truth', is always sourced in the mysterious encounter with the person of Jesus Christ, and so, while not primarily a deposit of revealed propositions, does lead to the development of doctrine and dogma.

Inspired also by Pope Paul VI in his encouragement of dialogue in *Ecclesiam Suam* (1964) the council again and again – and not least in its Pastoral Constitution on the Church in the Modern World, *Gaudium et Spes*, made clear its desire to be open to the world and to other Churches and faiths. This openness was rooted in what we share in common as human beings, as was made clear from the famous opening lines of *Gaudium et Spes*: 'The joys and the hopes, the griefs and the anxieties of the men and women of this age, especially those who are poor or in any way afflicted, these too are

13 Ibid., 36.
14 For what follows, as well as O'Malley, McBrien and O'Hanlon, op. cit., see in particular D. A. Lane (ed.), *Vatican II in Ireland, Fifty Years On,* Bern: Peter Lang, 2015; Jim Corkery SJ, '"Our Own Hope Had Been … " (Lk 24: 21): The Promise of Vatican II – Reality or Illusion?' in Suzanne Mulligan (ed.), *Reaping the Harvest: Fifty Years after Vatican II,* Dublin: Columba Press, 2012, 13–37; and Niall Coll (ed.), *Ireland and Vatican II,* Dublin: Columba Press, 2015.
15 O'Malley, op. cit., 95.

the joys and the hopes, the griefs and the anxieties of the followers of Christ' (GS, 1). And in this dialogue of shared humanity the council declares that the Church hopes to teach and help, but also to learn from and be helped by, the world (GS, 40–45).

The other major conciliar document on the Church, The Dogmatic Constitution on the Church, *Lumen Gentium*, articulates the mystery of the Church in terms of the People of God, a communion mirroring the inner life of the Blessed Trinity, and a sign of hope for the world. This hope springs from the pilgrim nature of this People's journey towards the reconciliation of unity-in-diversity, solidarity and collegiality that characterise the life of God and towards which the Holy Spirit leads both the Church and humankind in general. In this sense the Church is there not for its own sake but for the Kingdom. There is a universal call to holiness within the Church, and the language of first- and second-class ecclesial citizenship is dropped.

In particular the lay faithful, through Baptism, share in the priestly, prophetic and kingly office or role of Jesus Christ himself, both within the Church itself and in relation to the secular world. Moreover it is the People of God as a whole in whom the charism of inerrancy resides (LG, 12). It is within this subordinate context that the role of the hierarchy, including that of the papacy, is to be understood: the hierarchy exists to serve the whole People of God, not the other way around.[16] And so, as Orsy puts it,[17] the Church is not a military organisation where the highest in rank command and the rest obey – the notion of *communio* pertains to all levels of ecclesial life, based on the common baptism possessed by all, so that authority is to be exercised within the call of one mind and heart, and with respect for the inherent rights of the faithful, laity, priests, bishops and pope.

But a summary like the one just given tells only one half of the story. In fact the positions just described were hotly debated and all kinds of qualifiers were inserted to different conciliar texts in order to satisfy the concerns of a determined minority around

16 McBrien, op. cit., 166.
17 Op. cit., 8.

continuity with previous teaching, and hence to gain consensus. In particular O'Malley notes how '... collegiality would become the lightening-rod issue of the council',[18] and there was a vigorous debate throughout between those who, in today's parlance, wanted a 'hard collegiality' as opposed to those who wanted a 'soft' version. The texts themselves often simply leave statements about collegiality side-by-side with pre-conciliar statements about papal primacy and infallibility without any real reconciliation, and so are open to various interpretations. The Preliminary Explanatory Note (*Nota Explicativa Praevia*), a somewhat complex and ambiguous interpretation of collegiality that in effect gave succour to those who wanted a 'soft' version of collegiality, was introduced at a late stage of the drafting process of *Lumen Gentium* at papal behest. And so the bishops left the final session of the council with a sense, among most of them, that significant change had occurred, but with sufficient textual ambiguity and ongoing resistance to leave as an open question the actual implementation of this change.

In retrospect – and this is of crucial importance for what is going on in the Church today – it would seem that while there was significant cultural and theological development at the Second Vatican Council, nonetheless there was insufficient structural, legal and institutional grounding of many of the changes envisaged, in particular those concerning a more collegial Church at all levels. O'Malley observes that the majority side in the council, in favour of change, '... assumed an easier translation of ideas from the scholars' study to the social reality of the church than proved to be the case'.[19] The majority was consistently frustrated in its efforts to make its will felt through the establishment of real structural changes. It sometimes seemed to think that winning an affirmation of certain principles in the face of opposition to them would ensure their implementation.[20]

And so, in the particular issue of the relationship between the centre and the periphery, the Roman Curia, charged with implementing a reform that they had opposed in the council, was unequal to this task

18 O'Malley, op. cit., 163.
19 Ibid., 292.
20 Ibid., 312.

without itself being reformed. The Synod of Bishops, which might have acted as a counter-weight in favour of reform, was conceived by Paul VI in way that '… severed collegiality, the doctrine empowering the periphery, from institutional grounding'.[21] And so, collegiality, the linchpin in the centre-periphery relationship promoted by the majority, '… ended up an abstract teaching without point of entry into the social reality of the church. It ended up an ideal, no match for the deeply entrenched system'.[22] It is significant also in this context, and in the context of unresolved tensions still alive in today's Church, that the three issues regarded as so sensitive and potentially explosive by Paul VI that he withheld them from the council's agenda were clerical celibacy, birth control and the reform of the Roman Curia.

It is, finally, worth noting at this point how much of this analysis of the situation of the Church before and during the council relates so very clearly to the agenda of Pope Francis with his unapologetic return to the council's teaching for today's Church. Will we as Church be more receptive this time around? One thinks of the oft-quoted description of the Good Friday Agreement as 'Sunningdale for slow learners'!

After the Council [23]

The years immediately following the Second Vatican Council were a time of great excitement and hope, but also considerable turmoil in the Catholic Church. The changes brought about by the council were most apparent in the greater liturgical participation of the laity, not least by the use of the vernacular, the gradual flourishing of lay ministries in some parts of the world, and the redesign of churches to convey a more inclusive feel. However, with the new openness to question and imagining a different type of Church, there was also a surge of men and women leaving the religious life and priesthood, as well as hotly contested debates around sexuality and, later, gender. Historian and theologian Massimo Faggioli notes how some

---

21 Ibid., 311.
22 Ibid., loc. cit.
23 See Massimo Faggioli, *Vatican II, The Battle for Meaning,* Mahwah, NJ: Paulist Press, 2012, and Richard Gaillardetz, *An Unfinished Council,* Collegeville, MN: Liturgical Press, 2015.

historians distinguish an age of 'euphoria' which lasted about ten years until 1975, followed by a decade of 'contestations', and then concluded by what he (in 2012) described as the 'current period of *"restauration"'*, which had begun well before 2005.[24]

Whatever the periodisation one takes, there are some important landmarks and trends which bear on our present discussion about the future direction of Church in our own time of crisis. Even within the early period referred to by Faggioli he himself notes that '... it can be argued that the honeymoon period between the Council, the pope, and mainstream culture lasted even less than ten years'.[25] He is referring here to the encyclical *Humanae Vitae*, promulgated by Paul VI in 1968. Leading up to this encyclical it seemed that the Church was being prepared for a change to its own teaching on birth control. However, the Pope went against the advice of his own commission, apparently convinced by the argument that the change in question would be discontinuous with the tradition in an untenable way.

Whatever one thinks about the rights and wrongs of the issue itself – and many, even those who disagreed with the encyclical on the birth control issue itself still saw much that was prophetic in the document – this was a significant landmark decision. It signalled a return to centralised, papal decision-making in contrast to the more collegial model proposed at the council. It weakened the influence of the teaching authority, the Magisterium, among the majority of Catholics who found that they could not 'receive' the decision in good conscience. And it signalled to them and to the wider world that there was a serious disconnect between the Church at official level and contemporary culture in this most intimate of areas concerning human existence.

Nonetheless, this early period was also marked by a cautious decentralisation in some instances and the flourishing of the Church in some local regions. In this context one thinks of the Synod of Bishops in 1971 which named justice as a constituent element of

24 Massimo Faggioli, 'The Future of Vatican II', in Anthony Ciorra and Michael W. Higgins (eds), *Vatican II, A Universal Call to Holiness*, Mahwah, NJ: Paulist Press, 2012, 7–26, at 8.
25 Ibid.

the gospel and called for a congruence between Church teaching and its own intra-Church conduct in this area. Similarly the issue of justice was to the fore in the flourishing of the Latin American Church, Liberation Theology and the Conference of Bishops there (CELAM).

In what Faggioli describes as the period of contestation up to about 1985 (the date of the extraordinary synod convoked to assess the council twenty years on) there was the curious contrast between the hugely admired stance of Pope John Paul II on many social issues (not least in his role opposing Communism in his own native Poland, with wider consequences for the ultimate demise of Communism as then existing) and his progressive social encyclicals, and his seeming disregard for justice matters within the Church itself. It quickly became evident that the Church was becoming more and more centralised, that papal power was reasserting itself. In this he was helped greatly by Cardinal Joseph Ratzinger, who had been regarded as being on the progressive side of the conciliar debates, but who in post-conciliar times regretted what he saw as the rupture with tradition that was occurring in the Church. Ratzinger was to the forefront of the more conservative Communio group of theologians in the post-conciliar period, opposed the Concilium group, and, as Prefect of the Congregation of the Doctrine of the Faith, gave John Paul the theological support required to buttress a more centralised approach.

So, through the 1980s and into the 1990s in particular, a whole host of interventions occurred which far from implementing the collegial thrust of the council actually reversed it.[26] One thinks, for example, of how the revised Code of Canon Law (1983) not only failed to vindicate the rights of the faithful as articulated by the council, but also in one important respect actually reversed even the pre-conciliar situation (in its exclusion, in Canon 129, of the laity from their time-honoured right to engage in major decision-making processes). Similarly, with respect to bishops and their conferences, instead of the empowerment which the council envisaged, what has happened for the most part is that intermediate bodies have been weakened

26 See in particular Orsy, op. cit., 102-3, and all of chapter 7.

while Rome has strengthened its control – episcopal conferences, for example, have no genuine corporate power according to the *motu proprio* of John Paul II in 1998 (*Apostolicos Suos*). This letter allows for 'affective' but not 'effective' collegiality. And in another *motu proprio* from the same year (*Ad tuendam fidem* – to protect the faith, 1998), a new category of defined teaching ('definitively taught') is introduced, which an accompanying commentary claims to extend to such areas as the invalidity of Anglican Orders and the ordination of women. The latter issue was thus effectively withdrawn from public discussion.

The sense of Congar's 'creeping infallibility' was deepened by the way the Church handled disputes concerning doctrinal matters in these years. Despite an attempt to modernise the ecclesiastical procedures and rules in 1997, the CDF's way of proceeding was seen to be harsh – for example, in the attitude to Liberation Theology in general (many of whose insights did, however, succeed over time in making their way into official Roman teaching), and to many theologians in particular, including of course several Irish clerical voices. After a forensic examination of the 1997 Regulations Ladislas Orsy has this to say: 'A conclusion emerges in stark simplicity ... the Regulations do not respond, as they were intended to, to the demands of the present day ... they were not born from the vision of human dignity and the respect for honest conscience that is demanded in the world over today.'[27]

The papacy of Benedict XVI saw the publication of many deeply reflective and scholarly documents, not least on secularisation, its origins and its challenges. It was also characterised by continuing acrimony over the interpretation of the Second Vatican Council, under the rubric of a hermeneutic of continuity opposed to a hermeneutic of discontinuity or rupture. Benedict himself, as befitted the fine scholar that he is, was not (as many of his supporters supposed) formally categorisable under the rubric of 'continuity'. He argued, rather, for a hermeneutic of reform, happy to concede that change did indeed occur in Church teaching and practice, but only in matters that were contingent and historically bound, never

27 Ibid., 102–3.

in what was true in principle.[28] Nonetheless the impression given was of 'restoration', a 'reform of the reform', and constant use of the model of Church as *communio* (with more focus on its divine origin in the Trinity and less on the human structures that would be required to make communion and co-responsibility real). The absence of reference to the People of God model served to reinforce that impression.

It is important, however, to note finally two major contributions of John Paul II and Benedict XVI to the implementation of the Second Vatican Council. In 1995 John Paul II published the Encyclical *Ut Unum Sint*, in which, in an ecumenical context, he asked for help '… in heeding the request made of me to find a way of exercising the primacy which, in no way renouncing what is essential to its mission, is nonetheless open to the new situation … that we may seek – together of course – the forms in which this ministry may accomplish its service of love recognised by all concerned' (UUS, 95–96). This request by the Pope for help in re-envisaging the papacy has had a considerable response in theological circles. It does of course resonate with the concerns of the Second Vatican Council, and is apparent in the reflections and practice of Pope Francis.

In 2013 Benedict XVI resigned as pope. This bold gesture seems to have been due to a humble realisation that given the considerable challenges facing the Church, not least due to clerical child sexual abuse and the sense of scandal and chaos in the Roman Curia, and his own failing health, he simply was unable to do the job properly. The contrast with Pope John Paul II is striking: for several years his increased incapacity was obvious to all, and he died a very public death, offering his suffering for the redemption of the world. In a sense, then, John Paul II chose the way of the Cross, not least due to his belief in the institution of the Church and of the papacy. Can one say that, in contrast, Benedict's approach was more in line with the Incarnation, recognition of the weakness and limitation of all flesh, and of the reality that institutions exist for persons and not vice versa? However one considers it, there is no doubt that his unprecedented resignation had enormous symbolic significance,

28 Pope Benedict XVI, Address to the Roman Curia, 22 December 2005.

and resulted in a certain demystification of the aura or mystique surrounding the person and institution of papacy.

Conclusion

In his well-known work of the 1970s Avery Dulles, influenced by I.T. Ramsey and Thomas Kuhn in particular, had introduced the notion of 'models' in ecclesiology to throw light on the mystery of the Church.[29] He argued for the usefulness of several such models to do justice to the richness of the mystery involved, but noted that in effect it has often seemed that at different times in history one model became dominant and attained the status of a paradigm.[30] For a long time in Catholic ecclesiology this was the institutional model, on the analogy of the secular state, the *societas perfecta,* operating within a strictly hierarchical structure and a clear juridical code. Contemporary ecclesiologist Richard Gaillardetz refers to this model as 'the hierocratic form', drawing on the term 'hierarchology' coined by Yves Congar.[31] Dulles himself is clear that the institutional model cannot be taken as primary, arguing that institutions, while valuable and important, are subordinate to persons, and structures are subordinate to life.[32]

We have seen how the Second Vatican Council tried to balance out the institutional model of Church with a more collegial structure focused on the notion of the People of God. This is what Pope Francis now calls a synodal Church. And we have seen how – ironically, not least due to the lack of juridical, structural and institutional implementation – this model has failed for the most part to gain traction. Instead up to recently the Church has defaulted to the more centralist and hierarchical model in place for the best part of a millennium.[33]

It became clear from the start of his papacy that Francis believed he had a mandate to move towards a more collegial, synodal Church. This mandate came not least from his fellow cardinals after their

29 A. Dulles, *Models of the Church,* Dublin: Gill & Macmillan, 1987 (second edition).
30 Ibid., 29.
31 Gaillardetz, op. cit., 11.
32 Dulles, op. cit., 198.
33 Irish theologian Jim Corkery has put this failure in post-conciliar ecclesiology down to a 'failure of nerve' or even a 'loss of *faith*' – Corkery, op. cit., 30–32.

crisis discussions in the days leading up to his election. The old model of Church had proved unequal to the many challenges now presenting themselves. But why might a more collegial, synodal model be any more successful? Why is this discussion, and even dispute, over different models of the Church so important? The Irish context is instructive in this respect.

CHAPTER TWO

Background to the Crisis:
a Post-Catholic Ireland?[34]

*I think we can say that the once powerful, monolithic instiution
is being slowly disempowered, and what remains will need to be
re-shaped into a new, more culturally appropriate constellation.*
(Michael Conway, 'Faith-life, Church, and Institution',
The Furrow, September 2017)

In the middle of summer 2016, commenting on a controversy
surrounding the national seminary, St Patrick's College Maynooth,
Ireland's leading broadsheet *The Irish Times* had this to say in
an editorial: 'The Maynooth controversy would once have given
rise to major public disquiet. That it no longer does so reflects the
church's recent history. Many Catholics have long since abandoned
the institution – its princes, priests and politics – and are choosing to
interpret the faith according to their own conscience'.[35]

Coincidentally, earlier that year, an academic study in the field of
the sociology of religion was published with the title 'Transforming
Post-Catholic Ireland'.[36] The author, Gladys Ganiel, in explaining
her choice of title, refers explicitly to an article written in 2013 by
Archbishop Diarmuid Martin of Dublin, entitled 'A Post-Catholic
Ireland?'[37]

---

34 For what follows see Gerry O'Hanlon, 'The Catholic Church in Ireland Today', *Studies*, 106,
spring 2017, 9–20, originally published in *La Civiltà Cattolica*, n. 3998 (14/28 January 2017),
161–74; and O'Hanlon, 'Vatican II as a Resource for the Renewal of the Church in Ireland in
the Twenty-First Century', in Dermot A. Lane (ed.) *Vatican II in Ireland, Fifty Years On*, Bern:
Peter Lang, 2015, 219–36.

35 *The Irish Times*, 2 August 2016.

36 Gladys Ganiel, *Transforming Post-Catholic Ireland, Religious Practice in Late Modernity*,
Oxford: Oxford University Press, 2016.

37 Diarmuid Martin, 'A Post-Catholic Ireland? Renewing the Irish Church from Within',
America, The National Catholic Review, 20 May 2013.

Ganiel defines a post-Catholic Ireland in terms of 'a *shift in consciousness* in which the Catholic Church, as an institution, is no longer held in high esteem by most of the population and can no longer expect to exert a monopoly influence in social and political life'.[38] She argues that the future of faith in Ireland will depend on the development of 'extra-institutional' forms of religious expression (religion practised *outside or in addition to the institutional Catholic Church*[39]). Her analysis ties in with the frequently observed characteristic of modern Catholicism in Ireland – and indeed further afield – as becoming individualised and de-institutionalised. With the new emphasis on personal conscience as opposed to magisterial teaching, this is sometimes referred to as the 'Protestantisation' of the Catholic Church in Ireland.

Dr Martin himself has spoken and written frequently about the crisis confronting the Catholic Church in Ireland, warning that it ran the risk of becoming an 'irrelevant minority culture'.[40]

Historical background to the crisis

The traditional Catholicism which is now being superseded in Ireland had many distinguishing features.[41] It was a defining characteristic of Irish nationalism and identity, with a 'monopoly on the Irish religious market',[42] and had a strong relationship with state power, elevating the status of cleric to extraordinarily high levels and emphasising the evils of sexual sin. This was Catholicism with high levels of religious practice, a stress on rule-keeping and sin, a strong ethos of sacrifice and delayed gratification, a familiarity with austerity and a hope for fulfilment in the afterlife. It was characterised by a deep popular devotion featuring the likes of the rosary, benediction, sodalities, indulgences and processions. It provided comfort and fuelled the spiritual and ethical imaginations of its adherents, and had a deeply committed, global missionary

38 Ganiel, op. cit., 4.
39 Ibid., 21–24.
40 Diarmuid Martin: '"Keeping the Show on the Road": Is This the Future of the Irish Catholic Church?', address to the Cambridge Group for Irish Studies at Magdalene College, Cambridge, 22 February 2011.
41 For what follows see Ganiel, op. cit., chapter 2, and O'Hanlon, 'Vatican II as a source for the Renewal of the Church in Ireland', op. cit., 219–36.
42 Ganiel, op. cit., 3.

outreach. However, its un- and even anti-intellectual nature meant that it was ill-prepared for the challenges posed by a late-emerging modernity in Ireland. It was a religion in which the voice of the priest, the bishop and the pope could rely on formal authority to get a serious hearing, not just from the faithful, but also from the politician. A paternalistic ethos reigned and was almost universally accepted. Apart from the popular devotion already mentioned, this was Catholicism deeply institutional in form, dependent on a type of clericalism that was vulnerable to a more critical culture.

From the 1960s on this more critical culture emerged in Ireland. The influence of television and other media, economic development and increased urbanisation, foreign travel, EEC membership and enhanced educational opportunities all conspired to open Ireland up to the waves of critical questioning and secularisation already well advanced in many other parts of Europe. Internally the Church was at best lukewarm in its reception of the Second Vatican Council – there was liturgical change which was received for the most part positively, some increased lay involvement, including participation in various episcopal commissions established in the wake of the council, and a real energy around some issues of social justice (not least in the establishment of the still thriving developmental agency Trócaire, affiliated to the Irish Episcopal Conference). But the deeper teaching and spirit of the council (around Baptism and the role of the laity, collegiality, critical engagement with the world and the separation of Church and state) did not sufficiently penetrate the still somewhat complacent ethos of Irish Catholicism.[43]

The cracks became more visible from the 1980s on and have been widening and deepening since. In the 1980s the constitutional reform agenda of Taoiseach Garrett FitzGerald included the introduction of civil divorce to Ireland (eventually carried in a second referendum in 1995). It became obvious that particularly in the areas of sexuality and gender the stance of the bishops was increasingly at odds with that of the population in general – culminating in 2016 with the passing of the referendum on same-sex marriage.

43 See also Jim Corkery SJ, 'The Reception of Vatican II in Ireland', in Dermot A. Lane (ed.), *Vatican II in Ireland, Fifty Years On,* op. cit., 97–119.

In the meantime episcopal and ecclesial authority and reputation were severely damaged among a large segment of the population by the revelations, in the 1990s and the first decade of the millennium, of various clerical scandals (most notoriously the sexual abuse of children by clergy) and the poor handling of these scandals by those in authority as revealed in a number of public enquiries and reports. While these reports were often characterised by a lack of historical context and socio-cultural analysis, the egregious crimes they noted were undeniable and the effects were devastating.

In the short term they led to an almost aggressive attitude towards the Irish and universal Catholic Church, while in the longer term they have left a legacy of deep mistrust. It was after the publication of one such report (the Cloyne Report, 2011) that Taoiseach Enda Kenny referred in the Dáil to the 'dysfunction, disconnection, elitism and narcissism' in the Vatican, and there was a government announcement later that year that the Irish embassy to the Holy See was being closed (it was subsequently reopened in 2014). This was extraordinary from an Irish government and far from universally popular, but it was a sign of how far things had gone that the government felt free to use this kind of language and take this kind of action, satisfied that there would be sufficient popular support for doing so.

During this period,[44] while the figures of those self-identifying as Catholics remained high (84% identified as Catholic in the 2011 census, in contrast to a peak of 94.9% in 1961), religious practice, particularly among young and working-class people, declined (Mass attendance, for example, declined from 91% in 1971 to 35% in 2012, according to some estimates). The more recent 2016 census saw a drop in Catholics to the still very high figure of 78.3%, but with the number of people with no religion (atheists and agnostics) up to 10.1% (from 6% in 2011), the fastest growing sector in the population, and with an average age of thirty-four years (3.4 years younger than the population overall).[45] Obviously these figures admit of regional and urban/rural variation, but the trend is clear. It

44 Ganiel, op. cit., 25–53.
45 *The Irish Times*, 13 October 2017.

became evident also – as admitted by the Irish bishops themselves as part of their response to the recent Synod on the Family[46] – that increasing numbers of the faithful found difficulty with Catholic teaching in areas of sexuality and gender. Many women in particular – the backbone of the Irish Catholic Church – have long felt invisible and marginalised in their Church, and in a culture which is increasingly influenced by feminism and ideas of equality this has seemed unconscionable to many.

The Letter of Pope Benedict to Irish Catholics in the wake of the sexual abuse crisis and the subsequent apostolic visitation of seminaries and institutions of formation, while undoubtedly well intended and welcome, were widely felt not to have hit the mark and to have had a demoralising effect.[47] Similarly the cautioning, and in some cases removal from ministry, of a number of Irish religious has caused resentment in the Irish Church and public, not least by the perceived lack of due process. Vocations to the priesthood and religious life have sharply declined and various reform movements like the Association of Catholic Priests (ACP), the Association of Catholics in Ireland (ACI), We Are Church Ireland (WAC Ireland) and so on have sprung up.[48]

In this testing environment the Irish Episcopal Conference has found it difficult to respond in a way that shows confidence in its ability to supply the strong and wise leadership that is required in a situation of crisis. Theologian Eugene Duffy quotes from Karl Rahner's assessment of the German Church in 1971 and says that his description describes well the current situation in Ireland: 'The Church's public life even today (for all the good will that is not to be questioned) is dominated to a terrifying extent by ritualism, legalism, administration, and a boring and resigned spiritual

---

46 See Statement of the Irish Catholic Bishops' Conference regarding the questionnaire from the Synod on the Family, Thursday 13 March 2014, noting that 'many of those who responded to the questionnaire expressed particular difficulties with the teaching on extra-marital sex and cohabitation by unmarried couples, divorce and remarriage, family planning, assisted reproduction, homosexuality. The church's teaching in these sensitive areas is often not experienced as realistic, compassionate or life-enhancing'.
47 See, for example, Jim Corkery SJ, 'The Reception of Vatican II in Ireland Over Fifty Years', in Dermot A. Lane (ed.), *Vatican II in Ireland, Fifty Years On*, op. cit., 97–119, at 116.
48 See Brendan Hoban, *Who will break the bread for us?* Dublin: Banley House, 2013; Gabriel Daly OSA, *The Church, Always in Need of Reform*, Dublin: Dominican Publications, 2015.

mediocrity continuing along familiar lines.'[49]

The Catholicism that has been displaced in Ireland is the traditional one described above, in which a deep faith took the form of a strong institutional Church, with significant social and political prestige, whose paternalistic governance and teaching were carried out and received in a relatively uncritical way.

Faith does not disappear overnight, of course, and its traces remain over generations. Yet it can be seen that, especially among the young in Ireland, secularism has already made deep inroads, and even their undoubted social idealism often remains unconnected to the person of Jesus Christ, much less to the institution of the Church.

Some have argued that a way forward is to return to the more traditional form of Catholicism, even at the risk of becoming culturally irrelevant. This nostalgic turn, they would say, respects the mission of the Church to be counter-cultural and respects the fragile identity of younger Catholics in a post-modern world who require greater certainty. However, surely true tradition knows how to read the signs of the times, in fidelity with what went before, and to discern what in the culture is to be respected and used to reform the Church, as well as what is to be rejected?

Others place their hope in a religion that is entirely 'extra-institutional', putting their faith in Jesus and not the Church, and sharing the anti-institution and anti-establishment culture so prevalent in many other areas of contemporary life in the West. But, as the findings of social anthropologists indicate, institutions are necessary for human living; even 'extra-institutional' movements soon seek some institutional form, and are, in a sense, parasitic on the existence of institutions. The existence of the institution of the Church for Christians can be understood as altogether compatible with the law of the Incarnation and faithful to the teaching of Jesus Christ.

The classical debates within Catholic theology around the relationship between institution and charism (von Balthasar and Rahner), local and universal (Ratzinger and Kasper), centre and

---

49 Eugene Duffy, 'Reimaging the Church in Ireland in the Light of Vatican II', in Niall Coll (ed.), *Ireland and Vatican II*, op. cit., 113–29, at 126.

periphery (Congar and Liberation Theology), and indeed the legacy of the Second Vatican Council, offer a more hopeful reference point for a reform and renewal of the Irish Church in a way that may be both faithful to tradition and open to the signs of our times, culturally relevant. It is this conciliar legacy which Pope Francis so clearly recommends.

Cultural background to the crisis

It is tempting to look to the scandal of clerical child sexual abuse and its mishandling by Church authorities as the sole reason for the loss of influence by the Catholic Church in Irish life. However, historian Louise Fuller is surely correct in identifying the rapid emergence of secularisation in Irish society as being a crucial underlying factor.[50] Secularisation is a complex phenomenon and can have a variety of meanings, ranging from the increased separation of Church and state power, with abiding influence of religion on societal and cultural realities, through a relegation of religion to the private sphere, to an overtly secularist stance which involves a more direct denial of the existence of God and the transcendent and a demand that this become the default position of the state and society.[51] It is due to many philosophical, scientific, technological and economic changes brewing over many centuries and often beyond the Irish context.

It is this general cultural context which Baroness Nuala O'Loan addressed when, in a conference about the Church and education, she noted that teachers of children preparing for First Holy Communion and Confirmation 'have been aware for quite a while that the wider cultural shift away from religion has made passing on the faith an extremely difficult task'.[52]

Religious sociologists and theologians have noted and analysed this phenomenon. Tom Inglis, for example, in a recent qualitative

50 Louise Fuller, 'Revisiting the faith of our fathers ... and reimagining its relevance in the context of twenty-first century Ireland', in Eamon Maher and Eugene O'Brien (eds), *Tracing the Cultural Legacy of Irish Catholicism*, Manchester: Manchester University Press, 2017, 38–52.
51 Patrick Hannon, 'Church and State in Ireland: Perspectives of Vatican II', in Dermot A. Lane (ed.), *Vatican II in Ireland, Fifty Years On*, op. cit., 359–81; Iseult Honohan, 'Religious Perspectives and the Public Sphere', in Gerry O'Hanlon (ed.), *A Dialogue of Hope*, Dublin: Messenger Publications, 2017, 36–48.
52 *The Irish Catholic*, 19 October, 2017.

survey, found that only two of the hundred people he interviewed (a Muslim and an African Pentecostalist) said they were influenced by faith in their everyday decisions: for the rest family, friends and sports were much more spontaneously present in their hearts and minds and on their lips than any thought or mention of God. Inglis concludes that in general '... the institutional Church and Catholic language, beliefs and rituals are no longer significant webs of meaning in everyday life'.[53]

Dermot Lane has written perceptively about this phenomenon of secularisation.[54] Drawing on the analysis of Charles Taylor he notes that the process of secularisation (now well advanced in Ireland) has resulted in the emergence of a purely 'immanent frame' of reference, an 'exclusive humanism', a 'disenchanted universe' without reference to the transcendent. Within this new 'social imaginary' there has emerged, anthropologically, the notion of the modern 'buffered self', closed off from any transcendental horizon, increasingly critiqued by post-modernity, which, however, often fails to discover any objective traction and flounders in a fragile subjectivity. A common characteristic of modernity and post-modernity is a high esteem for freedom, often, however, limited to a reductively liberal notion of 'freedom from' without much agreement on what a 'freedom for' might look like.

This has happened rapidly in Ireland. If Matthew Arnold could already detect the ebbing tide of religion in mid nineteenth-century England ('The Sea of Faith ... But now I only hear its melancholy, long, withdrawing roar'), Gerard Manley Hopkins, later resident in Ireland, could still exultantly exclaim in 1877 that '... The world is charged with the grandeur of God', while Patrick Kavanagh, in the middle of the last century, could also say that '... God is in the bits and pieces of everyday'. It was left till much later in Ireland, to the genial Seamus Heaney, despite his abiding sense of the 'marvellous', to note that '... Christian myth is so contentious and exhausted'.[55]

53 Tom Inglis, 'Church and Culture in Catholic Ireland', *Studies*, 106, spring 2017, 21–30, at 24.
54 Dermot A. Lane, *Catholic Education in the Light of Vatican II and Laudato Si'*, Dublin: Veritas, 2015.

55 *The Irish Times*, 3 September 2013.

We are faced then, in Ireland, with the increasing reality of a 'God who is missing but not missed', of a culture that is often indifferent and sometimes hostile to Christianity and, in particular, to the institution of the Catholic Church. The challenge is to reawaken the need for salvation and the Good News of the gospels within a culture which experiences no such need. Parish priest Fr Joe McDonald puts it this way: 'I say things about cultivating a personal relationship with Jesus and they say "how can you cultivate a relationship somebody who died 2000 years ago?"'[56]

Maynooth theologian Michael Conway[57] has spelled out the implications of some of these cultural shifts for the institutional Church: we are living in a period when patriarchal, hierarchical institutions are being deconstructed – exclusively male leadership is being rejected; a pyramidal, hierarchical type of socio-cultural structure is yielding to one which is more egalitarian, with a challenging of a type of authority which does not offer reasons for decisions and policies. What is valued instead today is an alternative order, a new 'social imaginary', which is more horizontal, egalitarian, functional, discourse based, person centred and communitarian, and with enormous appreciation for the human person and authenticity. There is a 'rejection of insignificance' (de Certeau), referring to the previous silencing of marginalised voices in our culture (women, the LGBT community, children). In this context the life of faith must learn to listen, engage, enable, dialogue, critique respectfully, counter courageously and, at times, simply keep its own counsel – it respects the time and timing of the other. What is required in this new, evolving cultural matrix is less top-down command-and-obey type teaching, and more open space interaction nourished by the gospel and common life which facilitates an adult taking of responsibility for our lives of faith.

This shift in culture and practice is felt in particular among young people. Gerard Gallagher notes that 'millennials' (those born in the 1980s) are becoming an 'unconnected generation' – 'with an overall

---

56 *The Irish Catholic*, 5 October 2017.
57 Michael A. Conway, 'Ministry in Transition', *The Furrow*, 65, March 2014, 131–49; 'Christianity in Europe – a Future?', *The Furrow*, 65, July–August 2014, 331–338; New Beginnings and Painful Endings, *The Furrow*, 68, May 2017, 268–278, and especially 'Faith-life, Church, and Institution', *The Furrow*, 68, September 2017, 461–74.

Mass attendance weekly of around forty per cent or less, the under-fifties represent the first generation where the majority do not attend or practise their faith regularly. They are more inclined 'to go to Costa for coffee or to concerts than to church'.[58]

Gallagher goes on to posit the emergence of an Irish Church with three distinct parts – The Northern Church, which despite the inroads of secularisation, remains very religious (across the denominations) in all age categories, due in part to the coincidence of religion and identity; the Church in Leinster, where increasingly many young parents are likely to be under-catechised and have little or no faith commitment, with religion playing hardly any part in their lives, so that many Catholics in this region feel under pressure now to privatise their faith, and tell few they believe and belong to local parishes; the rest of Ireland, where traditional piety and progressive thinking are expressed by many people, and emerging voices in Church leadership in the West of Ireland, with, however, lower church attendance than in previous generations. We have reached the tipping point, where most of those claiming to be Catholics are no longer active in their faith. Contrasting statistics show that while almost eighty per cent of Irish people feel Catholic, large parts of towns and cities have regular participation of less than ten per cent. Gallagher concludes that the existing maintenance model of Church will not do in this context, that we must have a Church conversation to reimagine a different model of Church of intentional disciples.

Fuller[59] has an interesting proposal in this new cultural context. She suggests that the Church needs to look to artists to retrieve the religious imagination in an Ireland which, over sixty years,has gone from poverty and economic stagnation to the materialism of the Celtic Tiger, then economic meltdown, and now – I would add – a somewhat brittle recovery, in which it is far from clear that we have learned the kind of lessons which would lead to a more integral notion of the flourishing life. She notes the case of Seamus Heaney, whose own loss of faith, like that of many Irish people of his generation, occurred almost in passing, without explicit struggle,

58 Gerard Gallagher, 'Millennial Matters – Reconnecting the Disconnected', *The Furrow*, 68, September 2017, 479–87.
59 Fuller, op. cit., 47–50.

and yet whose poetry, paradoxically, continues to be suffused with
religious imagery:
There was never a scene
When I had it out with myself or with another.
The loss occurred off-stage. And yet I cannot
Disavow words like 'thanksgiving' or 'host'
Or 'communion bread'. They have an undying
Tremor and draw, like water far down[60]

Socio-economic background to the crisis
In a recent critique of Irish and global socio-economic development
a group of individuals with expertise in different fields of Irish life
diagnosed a crisis which challenges believers and non-believers
alike to a radical response.[61] The diagnosis noted that '... the model
of financial capitalism underlying the economic development since
the late 1970s had led to spectacular levels of inequalities of income
and wealth, ecologically catastrophic forms of growth, and the
dislocation of employment and income prospects for those employed
in manufacturing in the West'.[62] Public policy and institutions
have failed to protect populations from the negative consequences
of technological change, globalisation, mass migration and the
demographic change to ageing societies. The angry resistance to
this state of affairs has often led to nationalistic populism and a
coarsening of public discourse. However, the dominant form of
economic neo-liberalism has become hegemonic to such a degree
that it has shifted from being a framework for economic policy
to a comprehensive grounding for political rationality so that all
dimensions of human life become subject to market discipline.[63]
One symptom of this in Ireland is the persistence and deepening of
the housing crisis, which we are told is not so bad by international
standards, and yet has produced a grotesque crisis of homelessness,
while putting the long-established pattern of home ownership

60 Seamus Heaney, 'Out of this World', in *District and Circle*, London: Faber & Faber, 2006.
61 David Begg, Michael Cronin, Iseult Honohan, Dermot A. Lane, Dermot McCarthy, Fergus
    O'Ferrall, Gerry O'Hanlon SJ (eds), *A Dialogue of Hope, Critical Thinking for Critical Times*,
    Dublin: Messenger Publications, 2017.
62 Ibid., 13.
63 Ibid., 13–14.

beyond the capacity of young families.[64]

It is the contention of the group that the core values of this dominant paradigm are individualism, competitiveness, consumerism, a perception of the economy as the criterion of all value, the commodification of the aesthetic, and the pursuit of economic growth premised on the myth of unlimited resources.[65] These values are in marked contrast to republican ideals, which emphasise the participation of citizens, the pursuit of the common good and the recognition of interdependence.[66] The group expressed surprise that while – as the recent crash showed – this market ideology has proved itself to be the 'god that failed', the institutional response has not been to seek to dismantle a system that has generated hitherto unseen levels of inequality, greed and environmental destructiveness, but rather a return to an almost 'business as usual' model.[67] They conclude that the narrative supporting this status quo is spent, and we need to seek an alternative narrative and model which 'should have input from secular sources and religious voices, from poor people and rich people, from atheists and believers, from scientists and philosophers, from poets and theologians'.[68]

As we shall see, this analysis is not so far removed from that of Pope Francis, with his call for dialogue in order to address global and national ills which relegate the poor to the peripheries of life. If this approach is to bear fruit in Ireland, then it would seem that the Catholic Church, at hierarchical level, needs to reimagine its role as teacher and to move from an anxiously paternalistic mode of moral guardianship to a more Socratic, midwifery role of teaching as facilitating conversation between different groups in Irish society, learning from this conversation, and then seeking to persuade others (its own flock and those outside) of the cogency of whatever solutions may emerge.[69] The Church is, perhaps, already closer to this kind of approach in economic matters than in socio-sexual areas: one thinks, for example, of previous very helpful pastoral

64 Ibid., 21.
65 Ibid., 13.
66 Ibid., 14.
67 Ibid., 14.
68 Ibid., 26.
69 Ibid., 108–22.

letters of the bishops like *The Work of Justice* (1977) and *Work is the Key* (1992), which were the fruit of widespread consultation. However, given the loss of moral authority and given the cultural factors favouring participation and inclusion mentioned above, it would seem that more than ever the Catholic Church today needs to deepen its culture and practice of internal and external consultation, discussion and debate, if it hopes to gain traction in public debate in Ireland.

Conclusion

On a recent visit to Knock I was struck by the postures of the human figures in the magnificent apparition mosaic on the basilica wall: one with open mouth, others pointing to the sky, others still with bowed heads and clasped hands in adoration. I couldn't help but contrast this image of nineteenth-century unproblematic receptivity to transcendence with our own more contested context: bowed heads nowadays, in our digital age, are more likely to indicate a preoccupation with the marvels of manually held electronic devices.

I have indicated some of the features of this changed context, both in the universal Church and in Ireland. Michael Conway concludes his analysis of the link between this changed context and the future of the institutional Church by stating: '... I think we can say that the once powerful, monolithic institution is being slowly disempowered, and what remains of it will need to be re-shaped into a new, more culturally appropriate constellation'.[70] Today's culture is one which values inclusion and freedom, including freedom of speech, and views the exercise of authority and power in a much less deferential way than before, demanding participation and dialogue as part of how governance is exercised. North American historian Michael Lacy contrasts the pre-modern mode of governance in civil society (characterised by the rights of formal authority and the demands of unquestioning obedience) with the modern situation in which, when rules are laid down and decisions taken, '... grounds are prepared and referenced, rulings are accompanied by reasons and reassurances that relevant matters have been investigated,

70 Conway, 'Faith-life, Church, and Institution', *The Furrow*, op. cit., 474.

appropriate bodies of knowledge have been tapped, interested parties have been canvassed, and the likely consequences of the rule have been understood and prepared for'. He goes on to say: 'These are now among the customary duties of rule in civil society, and the need for something more closely comparable to them within the church is becoming increasingly evident'.[71]

The urgency of the present situation, particularly in Ireland, is highlighted by the shortage of priests, with a substantial critique by both Dermot Lane and Michael Conway of the notion that parish clustering is the only viable solution to the problem.[72] Clusters can have real value in offering combined resources to service common tasks such as administration and formation for laity, but they are no substitute for a vibrant local Eucharistic community. Can we begin to find a more radical approach more suited to the many challenges which face the Church, an approach which will allow the Church of our time to dialogue constructively with our world in that perpetual drama between faith and culture already apparent in Paul's conversations in the Athenian *Areopagus*, a major public square of his times?

It is this more radical approach which Pope Francis is offering. Drawing on the insights of the Second Vatican Council he is proposing to us a reform of the Church towards a more collegial, synodal culture and institution, which he believes is both more responsive to the signs of the times and yet faithful to the Church's own identity.

---

71 Michael Lacy, 'The Problem of Authority and its Limits', in Michael J. Lacy and Francis Oakley (eds), *The Crisis of Authority in Catholic Modernity*, Oxford: Oxford University Press, 2011, 1–25, at 9.
72 Dermot A. Lane, 'A Pastor looks Back and Forward', *The Furrow*, 68, October 2017, 547–553; Conway, 'Ministry in Transition', *The Furrow*, op. cit., 131–49.

PART TWO

Pope Francis
and the Quiet Revolution

CHAPTER THREE

The Main Lines
of Francis's Revolution

I invite everyone to be bold and creative in this task of rethinking the goals, structures, style and methods of evangelisation in their respective communities. (EG,33)

It may seem odd to speak of revolution and the papacy in the same breath, yet many commentators have been moved to do so by the words and actions of Pope Francis. North American theologian Richard Gaillardetz has spoken of a 'Copernican revolution' in terms of a Second Vatican Council rediscovery of a theology of the local Church.[73] Irish ecclesiologist Gerard Mannion speaks of an 'ecclesiological revolution', which, in privileging the model of Church as People of God, appears 'to be manifesting itself as another ecclesial instance of going "back to the future"'.[74] In the same vein, Paul Vallely quotes Italian Church historian Alberto Melloni as saying that the shift towards a more collegial form of Church government, represented in particular by the establishment by Francis of the Council of Cardinals, was '... the most important step in the history of the church for the past ten centuries'.[75] Vatican commentator Marco Politi may be taken to sum up this general perception: 'The word *revolution* is not out of place; it is a continuation of the great shift heralded by the Vatican II council.'[76]

Francis has made it clear that he unequivocally accepts the

---

73 Richard R. Gaillardetz, Conclusion, in Thomas P. Rausch SJ and Richard R. Gaillardetz (eds), *Go Into the Streets! The Welcoming Church of Pope Francis*, New York, NY: Paulist Press, 2016, 177.
74 Gerard Mannion, 'Re-Engaging the People of God', ibid., 71.
75 Vallely, op. cit., 184.
76 Politi, op. cit., xii.

teachings of the Second Vatican Council, in particular its collegial thrust in terms of ecclesiology, and has done so in a way that integrates the two conciliar documents on the Church, *Lumen Gentium* and *Gaudium et Spes*. The latter deals with the *ad extra* dimension of the Church (its relation to the world), the former with the *ad intra* dimension (the internal constitution of the Church). Francis has combined these two elements in a coherent and dynamic way.

He may have been helped to do this not least because, as a non-participant in the council itself, he has a less complex relationship with its teachings than former participants such as Paul VI, John Paul II and Benedict XVI. And, as a non-European, it may also help that he has been less influenced by what we have seen were the often fraught and contested 'culture wars', waged mainly in Europe and North America. These 'wars' originated as a response around the legacy of the so-called sexual revolution of the 1960s, with official Catholic teaching (particularly in the wake of *Humanae Vitae*) occupying the space of the conservative right and in opposition to the liberal left. They widened to include a more general attitude to the reception of the council under the rubric of a hermeneutic of continuity/discontinuity[77] between those who argued that nothing substantially new happened at the council and those who, in the words of historian John O'Malley, argued that something new had 'happened' there.[78] Francis simply refuses to engage in this 'war': instead he simply accepts the council as the inspiration of the Holy Spirit and seeks to implement it.

Mission

Many of us who have argued for Church reform over a long number of years have been helped by the insight of Francis that reform is not for its own sake – a kind of organisational purism – but is always functioning with resect to mission, which, in turn, is rooted in our encounter in faith with Jesus Christ.[79]

77 See Massimo Faggioli, *Vatican II, The Battle for Meaning*, Mahwah, NJ: Paulist Press, 2012, and *Pope Francis, Tradition in Transition*, New York, NY: Paulist Press, 2015.
78 John O'Malley, *What Happened at Vatican II*, Harvard, MA: Harvard University Press, 2008.
79 Gerry O'Hanlon, 'The Reform of the Church in her Missionary Outreach', in *Performing the Word, Festschrift for Ronan Drury*, Enda McDonagh (ed.), Dublin: Columba Press, 2014, 81–86.

This point, already apparent in his Interview with the Jesuit journals (Interview, September 2013), emerges clearly in his Apostolic Exhortation *Evangelii Gaudium* (November 2013). This document was written at the request of the Fathers of the 2012 Synod of Bishops on The New Evangelisation and it is clear that the documents of the Second Vatican Council on the Church, the Apostolic Exhortation *Evangelii Nuntiandi* of Paul VI (1975) and the *Aparaceida Document* of the Conference of Latin American and Caribbean Bishops (CELAM) of 2007 are major influences. This latter document was co-authored by the then Cardinal Bergoglio, with the inductive reading of the signs of the times characteristic of the Latin American approach.

Francis puts our faith encounter with Jesus at the centre of everything for Christians.[80] This encounter leads to discipleship and mission – '… that was the marvellous experience of those first disciples, who upon encountering Jesus were fascinated and astonished at the exceptional quality of the one speaking to them, especially how he treated them, satisfying the hunger and thirst for life that was in their hearts'.[81] Francis speaks eloquently of the 'joy of love',[82] a love which, however, is intrinsically outward, missionary focused – 'What kind of love would not feel the need to speak of the beloved, to point him out, to make him known?' (EG, 264).

Our encounter with Jesus in love is, above all, an encounter with the God of mercy, a mysterious personal encounter which may not be reduced to propositional language only. So, while doctrine, dogma and law have their place in the mission of Christians, Francis stresses also that in our relationship with God who is 'always greater', always a surprise, we can make mistakes, there is uncertainty, there is room for questioning and doubt in our quest for God, so that '… uncertainty is in every true discernment that is open to finding confirmation in spiritual consolation' (Interview). If moral teaching in particular becomes an obsession with '… the disjoined transmission of a multitude of doctrines to be insistently

---

80 For what follows see especially *Evangelii Gaudium*, 19–49, and Interview.
81 *Aparaceida Document*, 244.
82 Further developed, of course, in his later Apostolic Exhortation *Amoris Laetitia*, 2016, in which the parallels and interconnections between divine and human love are explored.

imposed' (EG, 35), disconnected from the heart of the gospel which is 'the beauty of the saving love of God made manifest in Jesus Christ' (EG 36), then the 'edifice of the Church's moral teaching risks becoming a house of cards' (EG, 39), likely to fall (Interview).

In this context what the Church needs most today in its mission is 'the ability to heal wounds and to warm the hearts of the faithful' (Interview), to be a Church which is like a 'field-hospital' (Interview), going out to street corners, a 'poor church for the poor' (EG, 198), a Church which 'attracts', with leaders who are not motivated by the ambitious careerism of clericalism, but who reek of the 'smell of the sheep' (EG, 24), and are not afraid of tenderness, are close to the flock.

It is part of the mission of the Church too, of course, to make known Jesus Christ as the source of hope and joy for the world. Francis is aware that this is a difficult challenge, in particular in those parts of the world which are heavily influenced by secularist trends.[83] An 'ever watchful scrutiny of the signs of the times' and a discernment of spirits (EG, 51ff) will reveal that these trends, at their best, contain much good with which the Christian can concur and learn from. So, for example, the Church needs to find a more incisive and visible role for women (EG, 103–4).[84] However, these trends are often accompanied by less desirable tendencies.

These include a culture which tends to relegate religion to the private sphere only, with an individualism which neglects the common good, and with a denial of the transcendent which can easily result in a moral relativism and superficiality which are easy prey to the consumerist mentality encouraged by modern capitalism. This latter involves an economic model which is characterised by exclusion, an idolatry of money, a financial system which rules rather than serves, and an inequality which spawns violence and is the root of social evils (EG, 202). Migrants, among many others, are victims of the 'globalisation of indifference' (LG, 54) which results from the toxic mix of this cultural and economic model. In his later encyclical letter *Laudato Si'* (2015) Francis makes it clear

83 *Evangelii Gaudium*, 50–109 for what follows.
84 See Chapter Eight for a fuller treatment of this important topic.

that the socio-economic crisis, ultimately rooted in a crisis of faith, is not separate from the ecological crisis (LS, 139) and calls for an 'integral ecology' which would unite all dimensions (LS, chapter 4 in particular).

Mission demands reform

In taking this comprehensive approach to mission, and to its source in faith, in our encounter with Jesus Christ, Francis is true to the insight of the Second Vatican Council that the Church does not exist for its own sake, but rather as a kind of sacrament (LG, 1) of Jesus Christ and of God's kingdom for the world. And it is because of this profoundly outward, 'centrifugal'[85] nature of the Church that Francis can hope that its missionary impulse will be 'capable of transforming everything, so that the Church's customs, ways of doing things, times and schedules, language and structures can be suitably channelled for the evangelisation of today's world rather than for her self-preservation' (EG, 27). This is a Church which needs to be in dialogue, with the world and internally. He notes, in particular, that the consequent renewal of structures is 'demanded' by pastoral conversion (EG, 27).

The starting point and core of the project of Francis to renew and reform the Catholic Church is, then, one of faith: and this has the potential to unite both liberals and conservatives.

What does reform involve?[86]

Pope Francis completed the fifth anniversary of his pontificate in March 2018. Media commentary in Ireland and elsewhere tends to focus on more visibly immediate areas of interest surrounding his papacy – his pastoral style, the opposition to his teaching on the admission of divorced and remarried Catholics to communion, his attempts to tackle clerical sexual abuse of children (mediated in particular through the experience of Marie Collins), his reform of the Vatican Curia and of Vatican finances, the dissatisfaction in

85 Christopher Ruddy, 'The Local and Universal Church', in Rausch and Gaillardetz (eds), op. cit., 109–24, at 112.
86 For what follows, see Gerry O'Hanlon, 'Ireland and the Quiet Revolution in the Catholic Church', *The Furrow*, 68, May 2017, 259–267.

many quarters around the method of appointing bishops, and the shortage of priests. Referring to this latter point in Ireland, the former Papal Nuncio, Archbishop Charles Brown, was reported in March 2017 as saying: 'We're at the edge of an actuarial cliff here, and we're going to start into a free fall'.[87]

All these – and many other – particular issues are of great importance, but arguably they do not identify the underlying core of what Francis is attempting to do with the Catholic Church. As we have seen, many theological and media commentators abroad have spoken of a revolution. I want to explore here the main lines of his core revolution and its strategy, a strategy which is crucial in influencing almost all the particular issues mentioned above.

Francis and Church Synodality in the Third Millennium

Francis himself described the Apostolic Exhortation *Evangelii Gaudium* as 'programmatic' (EG, 25). Throughout this document his focus is very much on 'initiating processes rather than possessing spaces' (EG, 223 – 'time is greater than space' – 222–25). What he means by this somewhat cryptic phrase is that 'we need to give priority to actions which generate new processes in society and engage other persons and groups who can develop them to the point where they bear fruit in significant historical events' (EG, 223). In other words, Francis is convinced that radical change is not the same as 'obtaining immediate results which yield easy, quick short-term political gains' (EG, 224), but is more likely to emerge from a more patient and genuinely inclusive process. It is also more likely to emerge from the 'peripheries' in its ongoing relationship with the 'centre' – 'I am convinced of one thing: the great changes in history were realised when reality was seen not from the centre but rather from the periphery'.[88]

When one translates this conviction into the ecclesial sphere Francis spells out very clearly[89] that what is required for the third

87 *The Irish Times*, Saturday, 18 March 2017.
88 Pope Francis, 'Wake up the World', Conversation with Religious, November 29, 2013 – see *La Civiltà Cattolica*, 2014, I, 3–17, for original text.
89 See in particular his address commemorating the fiftieth anniversary of the establishment of the Synod of Bishops, 17 October 2015.

millennium is a 'synodal Church', with a sound decentralisation, in which there is free and open debate and consultation. In this new context the pope acts as head of, but also as a member of, the college of bishops, and a reformed Roman Curia sees itself at the service of the whole Church (in particular of the pope together with the bishops). Again, in this new paradigm, collegiality is to be present at all levels of the Church. This will mean that more effective authority is given to national and regional episcopal conferences. It will also mean that the 'voice of the faithful', and the role of the baptised as sharers in the priestly, prophetic and kingly offices of Jesus Christ, are clearly brought to bear at local, intermediate and universal levels. This implies some lay involvement both in governance and in the formation and reception of teaching at all levels of the Church.

Why the term 'synodal'?
The terminology used to describe this 'inverted pyramid'[90] way of looking at the Church centres around two words in particular – 'synodality' and 'collegiality'. To many Irish Catholic ears the term 'synodal' is a little difficult and unfamiliar and may, dimly, convey a certain 'Protestant' feel. This is no coincidence: Francis explicitly praises the Orthodox for retaining this traditional culture and structure of the Catholic Church ('from them we can learn more about the meaning of episcopal collegiality and the tradition of synodality' – Interview, and see also EG, 246), and notes that 'the commitment to build a synodal church to which all are called … is loaded with ecumenical implications' (Address). This synodal tradition has also been kept alive among many of our Protestant fellow Christians.

In a helpful conceptual clarification Ladislas Orsy notes that 'collegiality is a Latin legal term and in Western ecclesiology it refers to the external constitutional structures and operations of a corporate body. Eastern Christians prefer to speak of 'synodality', which is a Greek theological term and signifies an invisible unity created in 'those of the road together'… by the indwelling Spirit'. Orsy goes

---

90 See Ormond Rush, 'Inverting the Pyramid: The *Sensus Fidelium* in a Synodal Church', *Theological Studies*, 78, June 2017, 299–325.

on to suggest that 'it would be a wholesome theological position – both in the East and the West – to hold that synodality, 'being on the road together', generates collegiality, 'getting together'. The invisible communion is incarnated in visible operation', and he recalls that all this is true to the advances made in synodality/collegiality in the Second Vatican Council where '... the conciliar discourses, debates and battles were part and parcel in a process of "development of doctrine"'.[91]

Australian theologian Osmond Rush offers a further clarification. He notes that collegiality is often used in a limited sense to speak of the relationship between papal primacy and the role of the bishops.[92] What Francis intends is 'an entirely synodal church', so that, as Archbishop Mark Coleridge of Melbourne put it, synodality means 'not just some of the bishops some of the time but all of the Church all of the time'. Rush goes on to note that '... the Pope is using "synodality" as a neat catch-all phrase for how Vatican II envisioned the church *ad intra* (with significant implications for how it envisioned the church *ad extra*), and in a way that goes beyond what the council explicitly stated regarding synods'.[93]

The Practice of Francis

It is clear that this synodal practice is what Francis has been doing since the start of his pontificate. He has located himself primarily as bishop of Rome, within the College of Bishops, and has attempted to give institutional form to this ecclesial and papal reform by working together with a council of cardinals, by renewing the effective authority of the Synod of Bishops, and by urging local and regional episcopal conferences and individual bishops to assume their responsibilities to govern their own dioceses, always in consultation with the faithful.

91 Ladislas Orsy, 'Where is Our Church Going? searching for a response', *The Furrow*, 63, December 2012, 591–5, at 593.
92 Rush, op. cit., 303–5. This distinction between synodality (involving all members of the church) and collegiality (the specific form in which ecclesial synodality manifests and realises itself through the ministry of bishops) is confirmed by the International Theological Commission document Synodality in the Life and Mission of the Church, 2018 – see Joshua J. McElwee, 4 May 2018 – https://www.ncronline.org/news/vatican/consult-laity-vatican-theological- commision-says
93 Ibid., 304.

This decentralisation of governance is to be in communion with the rest of the Church of course, but requires bishops to be particularly attentive to the signs of the times in their own spheres of authority, so that, as bishops, they will sometimes be ahead of their flocks, sometimes walking alongside and sometimes following along behind, and all the time consulting and listening, not least to those who tell them things they may not want to hear (EG, 31). This turn to a more locally grounded, less centralist model of Church is confirmed in the Papal Apostolic Exhortation *Amoris Laetitia*, fruit of the synodal process, where it is stated early on that '… not all discussion of doctrinal, moral or pastoral issues need to be settled by interventions of the magisterium' (AL, 2), and where it is clear anyway that the notion of Magisterium has been expanded in a much more inclusive way.

The worldwide consultation of the faithful, prior to and during the Synod on the Family, no matter how clumsily and unevenly carried out, was an important earnest of this transition to a more participative and inclusive Church. Francis claims that this synodal model is based on sound theological principles, the practice of the first millennium and the demands of contemporary culture. It has led already to a more open culture of debate within the Church and to that modest, if controverted, development of doctrine around the readmission of divorced and remarried people to communion contained in *Amoris Laetitia*.[94]

Vatican commentator Joshua J. McElwee notes the change in Church culture that the Pope is bringing about, 'playing a very long game, trying to shift the Church's vision of its mission and its stance towards the world'.[95] In the same article he writes that eminent moral theologian Lisa Sowle Cahill told him that the Pope used the synod process as a way to consider possible developments in church teaching without causing open divisions in the church, and that she went on to describe Francis as a 'wonderful ecclesial politician'. For Francis it is clear that ecclesial reform is always functioning with respect to mission, to our encounter with Jesus

94 See Gerry O'Hanlon, 'The Joy of Love, *Amoris Laetitia*', *The Furrow*, 67, June 2016, 328–36.
95 Joshua J. McElwee, 'Since 2013, Pope Francis has endeavoured to shift church culture', *National Catholic Reporter*, 9 March 2017.

Christ and his proclamation of the Kingdom of justice and peace already beginning in this world, Jesus who is the personification of God's mercy and love. At the heart of this reform lies a personal and communal discernment of what it is God wants of our Church now, a discernment that takes account in its formation of doctrine of the 'sense of the faithful' (not least popular piety and the voice of the poor), the voice of theologians, and the authoritative role of pope and bishops. It also allows for lay participation in Church governance. The potential for change in this more inclusive ecclesial way of proceeding is enormous.

Opposition

Another experienced Vatican commentator, Marco Politi, has written a forensic account of the opposition to Francis, the English translation of which takes the story up to 2015.[96] Tellingly, the title of Politi's book is *Pope Francis Among the Wolves,* with a sub-title *The Inside Story of a Revolution.* Politi states that 'Francis's revolution has a name: the missionary transformation of the Church',[97] and he identifies 'collegiality' as a principal pillar of this revolution.[98] He notes that the opposition to the attempted shift from an imperial, monarchical Church to one that is more synodal and collegial comes from many sources.

Among them are many in the Roman Curia who find change difficult and are accustomed to a clericalism which supports ambitious self-seekers, with many bishops and local hierarchies used to a more unthinking and less responsible role, including some people of power and even criminality (mafiosi in Italy and elsewhere) who are more at ease with a 'gospel of prosperity' and find the social gospel of Francis (articulated in *Evangelii Gaudium* and *Laudato Si'* in particular) hard to stomach and those who suspect that the move to synodality is a cover for changes in Church teaching with regard to gender and sexuality. Politi notes in particular the concerted opposition to Francis in Italy (where his changes are felt

96 Marco Politi, *Pope Francis Among the Wolves, The Inside Story of a Revolution,* New York, NY: Columbia University Press, 2015 (English translation).
97 Ibid., 127.
98 Ibid., loc. cit.

most keenly) and the United States, where, as Massimo Faggioli has noted, 'there exists a robust network of Catholic universities, colleges, and lobbies that, in parallel to conservative American Protestantism, consider a traditionalist outlook on faith essential to the moral health of the United States'.[99]

Since the book was published in 2015 we have seen this opposition harden and become more visible, with a campaign of street posters in Rome and the kind of bureaucratic obfuscation resistant to change highlighted by Marie Collins in her dealings with Roman Congregations (in particular the Congregation for the Doctrine of the Faith). In 2016 there was the open opposition to the Exhortation *The Joy of Love*, spearheaded by the four cardinals in their articulation of the '*dubia*', with the demand for 'yes or no' answers and a threat of 'fraternal correction' if the answers proved unsatisfactory. And in 2017 there was the 'filial correction' of the Pope's teaching by more than sixty conservative scholars and clerics, with suggestions that some of his positions represented 'material' if not 'formal' heresy.[100]

What is going on here? I think that, apart from understandable resistance to change, there is also a real fear that the acceptance of a synodal, collegial Church is a kind of Trojan horse which will inevitably, over time, usher in the kind of changes, the 'doctrinal development' referred to by Orsy and Cahill. These changes have already been foreshadowed in the relaxing of the rules around communion for divorced and remarried people arising out of the recent synod and they are anathema to a conservative minority. In this context Paul Vallely may express matters a little too polemically, but he is surely correct to point out that the doctrinal opposition to Francis is both exaggerated and on weak grounds (an 'impertinence'), given that the offending exhortation of Francis (*Amoris Laetitia*) in particular comes at the end of an intensive and wide consultation of the Church, and can be shown to be in accordance with both Scripture and Tradition.[101]

Francis himself may well be quite conservative himself doctrinally, but a more synodal Church (which listens to the voices of the

99 Politi, op. cit., 165.
100 Richard Gaillardetz, 'Is the Pope a Catholic?' *The Tablet,* 7 October 2017, 4–5.
101 Paul Vallely, 'So much to do, so little time', *The Tablet,* 11 March, 2017, 4–6, at 5.

faithful and of theologians) is surely bound to result in change and significant doctrinal development, as well as a form of governance more in touch with the realities and challenges of our world and less restricted by an exclusively clericalist imagination.

Clearly there is, and will be, significant opposition to this approach, and we will address the many legitimate concerns about what Francis is proposing in future chapters. But, suffice to say for now, if change can come about collegially, discerning together the promptings of the Holy Spirit, as opposed to monarchically (whether through a pope of the right or the left) and only in reaction to the protests of particular pressure groups, then there is a better chance of maintaining unity in the Church. A better chance too of moving from fear to hope, of facilitating individual and communal conversion in a way which allows conservative and liberals to find the greater unity that is anchored in their common love of Jesus Christ. This is the crux of the revolution of Francis, and while some individual issues (one thinks of the reform of Vatican finances and the safety of children) do demand urgent and singular attention, other important issues are best settled within the emerging process of synodality.

This process is illustrated, for example, by the papal *motu proprio,* an apostolic letter 'on his own responsibility', *Magnum Principium* (The Great Principle, December 2017), in which Francis (on foot of establishing a commission to investigate the matter) effectively moved to restore the norm of 'dynamic equivalence' as opposed to a word-for-word methodology when translating liturgical texts, and explicitly returns principal authority for such translations to episcopal conferences, as intended by the Second Vatican Council.[102] He is also encouraging a synod of the Church in the Amazon region in which the partial lifting of priestly celibacy will be up for debate, at the request of Cardinal Hummes, President of the Episcopal Commission of the Amazon. He has also set up a commission of men and women to study the feasibility of female deacons, an issue

102 In a press release on Wednesday 6 December 2017 the Irish bishops welcomed the pope's initiative and said they would 'give time to reflection and discussion' on its full implementation, working collaboratively with other episcopal conferences 'while giving full regard to the rights and responsibilities of the Bishops' Conference as affirmed by the Holy Father Pope Francis'.

with enormous repercussions for the wider, developing role of women in the Church.

Francis himself has remained serene and apparently unflappable in the teeth of the opposition. He welcomes open debate, and distinguishes between opposition which is principled and open, that which is malevolent and that which is covert.[103] He welcomes open opposition which is in good faith: it is through the clash of ideas in public debate that truth emerges. Public discussion in the context of communal discernment has a way of laying bare the 'hidden secrets of the heart' (1 Cor 14: 25) and exposing the malice in opposition that is grounded in bad faith. And as to those who seem to be apathetic, Francis encourages engagement, in true Ignatian style, vis-à-vis those who seem to blow neither hot nor cold, an engagement which may reveal that what seemed like apathy is instead a form of passive aggression.

In a revealing 'Q and A' session with the Jesuits gathered for their General Congregation 36 in Rome in autumn 2016, Francis made it clear that this serenity is not due to any innate optimism: rather, he reveals, 'I am rather pessimistic, always!' and his serenity comes from that sense, at the end of each day, that 'I realise that I have been led', when 'I realise that despite my resistance, there was a driving force there like a wave that carried me along' and 'this gives me consolation'. He goes on to say: 'It is like a feeling, "He is here"'.[104] It is in this context of being led by the Lord that he listed the eighteen steps he has taken in the curial reform process up to the end of 2016 (among them the Council of Cardinals, the promotion of lay men and women within the Roman Curia, the decrees regarding negligent bishops and the reform of Vatican finances).[105]

Ecclesiologist Richard Gaillardetz has written helpfully about the shift under Pope Francis to the exercise of a more pastoral magisterium in the Church, characterised by service to a synodal, listening Church; by reliance on symbolic gesture more than

103 Gerard O'Connell, *America*, 22 December 2016.
104 General Congregation 26, 2016, Dublin: Messenger Publications, 2017, 71–85, at 81.
105 Joshua J. McElwee, *National Catholic Reporter*, 22 December 2016. See also, for an update of Politi's assessment, and, in particular, for his comment on ongoing resistance to the papal attempts to reform Vatican finances and procedures for clerical child sexual abuse, Marco Politi, 'Choppy Waters for the Ship of St Peter', *The Tablet*, 6 January 2018, 4–6.

juridical act; by commitment to the decentralisation of authority; by exhibiting an appropriate doctrinal humility; by acting through the practice of discernment and the formation of conscience; and by reluctance to pronounce prematurely on controverted issues.[106]

I would simply add that pastoral in this context should be understood to involve the relationship between faith/the Church and the world, but not as the antithesis of doctrinal. The attempt was made by some to reduce the Second Vatican Council to 'only a pastoral Council'. This is part of a classicist mentality that wants to consider doctrine as eternally unchanging, with a concession only to application. This attempt has been cogently rejected by many theologians operating within a more historically aware consciousness, among them Bishop Johan Bonny (there should not be an antithesis between the pastoral and doctrinal), Raphael Gallagher (theology does not consist in a first act of 'pure' or 'real' theology, followed then by a concessionary pastoral theology which involves a more merciful application of first principles – rather, there is a reciprocity between the two movements) and Edward Hannenberg (the doctrinal development that can emerge from properly discerned 'anomalies' in pastoral practice).[107] Indeed, elsewhere Gaillardetz himself is clear that 'while it is a common misconception that doctrinal change and development occur primarily by ecclesiastical fiat', in fact 'doctrine changes when pastoral contexts shift and new insights emerge such that particular doctrinal formulations no longer mediate the saving message of God's transforming love'.[108]

One of the more interesting points to emerge from Politi's analysis of the opposition to Francis is the extent to which it is rooted in inertia or apathy, in passive resistance or sometimes with a passive-aggressive mentality, rather than in overt hostility. He references the satirical wit of Italian comedian Maurizio Crozza in this context – his skit features Pope Francis plodding along the beginning of the Via Salaria at seven o'clock in the morning carrying a refrigerator on his

106 Richard Gaillardetz, 'Doctrinal Authority in the Francis Era, Toward a Pastoral Magisterium in Today's Church', *Commonweal*, 19 December 2016.
107 See O'Hanlon, 'The Quiet Revolution – Reflections on Synod 2015', *The Furrow*, 66, December 2015, 637–39; and 'The Joy of Love', *The Furrow*, 67, June 2016, 332.
108 Richard Gaillardetz, 'The Pastoral Orientation of Doctrine', in Rausch and Gaillardetz, op. cit., 125–40, at 137.

shoulder to give to a widow; Francis asks 'what door do we deliver to?' and one of his two splendidly dressed secretaries who don't lift a finger to help him answers 'Number 1321, Holiness'. A prostitute, groups of *ciellini* (members of *Communione e Liberazione)*, Roma football supporters and two cardinals come along and ask him for photos and blessings. The widow refuses the gift because it is the wrong colour. 'It could have been worse', murmurs Francis, as he sets off homeward.[109]

At the oral presentation of his book in the Loyola Institute in Trinity College Dublin Politi invoked another image to describe what is happening in the Church: Francis is like a star soccer player; many spectators admire him greatly, they urge him on – but very few get on the pitch with him to ensure victory. At their recent *Ad Limina* visit to Rome it was reported that Francis told the Irish bishops they had to be like goalkeepers, fielding balls from all angles. What kind of role is the Irish Catholic Church, bishops, priests and laity, playing to ensure that the Francis revolution gains ground?[110]

Conclusion

At the heart of any reform impulse, it seems to me, is an experience which may seem very remote from reform: I refer to that encounter with Jesus Christ which is the foundation of every Christian life. Think of Jesus saying to Mary Magdalene: 'Mary' (Jn 20:16). Think of his words to the Rich Young Man – 'he looked steadily at him, and he loved him' (Mk 10:21). Think of the words of the Father to Jesus at his Baptism and Transfiguration – 'This is my Beloved Son' (Mk 1:11 and 9:7). Think of the way the Hebrew Covenant (Old Testament) speaks of God's mercy and compassion in the physical terms of guts, heart, bowels – God is moved, deeply, loves us deeply and personally. Francis himself has made it clear that for him this encounter occurs in the context of God's mercy to him, a sinner, and cites his somewhat authoritarian exercise of power as a young Jesuit superior as one instance of his own sinfulness (Interview).

109 Politi, op. cit., 209–10.
110 Ibid., chapter 9.

Ideally all the baptised will have some experience of this deeply personal love in their lives, and out of it develops a real relationship which shapes all that we do. Reform attempted from this place is qualitatively different from reform springing from a systems management and organisation horizon alone, no matter how rightly fuelled by righteous anger and a zeal for justice. Our anger and justice are rooted in love: this is a rich, radical position, more capable of lasting and inclusive reform. Someone who feels and is loved is impelled to announce Good News, impelled to act in this spirit – and Luke in his Acts of the Apostles is replete with this sending of the Holy Spirit to transform the lives of the early disciples and their surrounding world.

Francis, following the Second Vatican Council, wants a Church which, as the People of God, comprises disciples converted by the merciful love of Jesus Christ to engage with our world in a missionary conversation and dialogue. This dialogue is respectful of the traces of the Spirit already present in other faiths, in those of no faith, in the groaning of creation (Rm 8:22) on our planet earth.

The paradigm for this Church will be far removed from the institutional model outlined by Dulles,[111] with its self-contained, juridical and propositional mode of revelation which required simple obedience from the faithful. Instead, rooted in the Second Vatican Council but learning from and bypassing the many contested developments since then, Francis is proposing a synodal model of Church, a process and way of being Church which, he believes, is consistent with the Christian tradition and is better attuned to the signs of our times.

This model involves the listening to many different voices. Many of those who oppose him fear that this can lead to a kind of Babel of chaos and discord. Francis, however, is confident that through a Spirit-led discernment of the many voices, with appropriate institutions and structures to support it, we are being led towards a new Pentecost in which the world is given meaning and hope, and the Church is renewed and reformed.

111 Dulles, op. cit., chapter 1.

CHAPTER FOUR

The Core of the Revolutionary Strategy

It is precisely this path of synodality which God expects of the
Church in the third millennium.
(Pope Francis, address to commemorate the fiftieth anniversary of the
institution of the Synod of Bishops, 17 October 2015)

The humorous notice which Pope Francis placed outside his door in the Vatican – *'non lamentarsi'*, don't whinge – was an attempt to remind Curial officials not to get obsessed with petty aggravations, but to keep in mind the bigger picture. Still, it is clear that part of this bigger picture is a response to what the cardinals had spoken about in their pre-conclave congregations, a 'heeding, receiving and responding to the Spirit encountered in the aspirations and laments of those suffering in the Church and in the world, and the wailing of our damaged environment'.[112] In other words, it is good to look reality in the eye, to lament lack of engagement and be angry at injustice, but it is also good to seek a positive response.

We have seen the main outline of the response of Francis, with its focus on a synodal Church, arising from our encounter in faith with Jesus Christ and the 'revolution of tenderness' (EG, 88) which this effects. A succinct presentation of his thoughts on this matter of synodality occurs in his October 2017 address, during the second session of the Synod of Bishops on the Family. This is the clearest, most concise account of what he means by adopting synodality as a way of being Church.

112 Bradford Hinze, 'Listening to the Spirit', *The Tablet*, 3 June 2017, 4–5; and *Prophetic Obedience, Ecclesiology for a Dialogical Church*, New York, NY: Orbis, 2016.

A synodal Church[113]
In this Address Francis reminds us of the biblical roots of synodality – a walking or journeying together, along the road of discipleship with Jesus, laity, pastors, the bishop of Rome. It is a legacy of the Second Vatican Council and is the pathway 'that God expects from the Church in the third millennium'. As he develops this notion in his address it is clear, as Rush points out, that this pathway refers not just to the formal institution and structure of the Synod of Bishops, which the Pope clearly wants to re-energise, but rather that the term 'synodal' is a catch-all phrase for a much wider practice of the walking together of the Pilgrim People of God, already envisaged in the Second Vatican Council. To this effect Francis notes in his Address that '... the Synod of Bishops, representing the Catholic episcopate, becomes an expression of episcopal collegiality *within an entirely synodal church* (my emphasis). Two different phrases: "episcopal collegiality" and an "entirely synodal church"'. This involves everyone – the commitment to build a synodal Church is 'a mission to which we are all called, each with the role entrusted by the Lord'.

At the centre of this vision is the notion of the Church as the People of God, the baptised faithful with their infallible 'supernatural sense of faith' (LG, 12) when there is a universal consensus in matters of faith and morals. This '*sensus fidei*' prevents any rigid separation between the teaching and learning Church, so that all the baptised have a role in discerning 'the new ways that the Lord is revealing to the Church' (Address). This means that 'all the baptised, whatever their position in the Church or their level of instruction in the faith, are agents of evangelisation, and it would be insufficient to envisage a plan of evangelisation to be carried out by professionals while the rest of the faithful would be passive recipients'. One can see how far the Church has travelled from the vision of Pius IX and Pius X and O'Malley's 'long nineteenth century'. But it is also important to note that while a committed, informed and educated faithful is obviously of value, still Francis is insisting here that all the faithful,

113 For what follows see Gerry O'Hanlon, 'The Quiet Revolution – Reflections on Synod 2015', *The Furrow*, 66, December 2015, 632–641.

irrespective of education, have a role, and elsewhere he will refer in particular to the special place of the poor and of popular piety in discerning the Spirit (EG, 69–70; 90; 120–6; 187; 191; 198).

It is precisely his conviction about this active role of the baptised – who share 'in the prophetic office of Christ' – that guided Francis when he 'desired that God's people would be consulted in the preparation of the two-phase synod on the family'. He quotes the time-honoured maxim of Roman and canon law in this context: *Quod omnes tanget ab omnibus tractari debet* (that which touches all should be dealt with by all). This consultation was a first attempt to hear the 'sense of the faith', and the path of synodality then proceeds by way of the bishops, including the particular role of the bishop of Rome, carefully distinguishing the true sense of the faith from that which 'flows from frequently changing public opinion'. (Chapter Five looks at how one can more precisely discern the true sense of faith.)

However, for now it is important to note how Francis acknowledges the right of all to be consulted in what affects all – a far cry from the more restrictive and deductive notion of a Magisterium whose special access to the supernatural does not require any listening to human experience. For Francis a listening process is central to how the Church should proceed, a listening which is more than just hearing but 'a mutual listening in which everyone has something to learn. The faithful people, the college of Bishops, the Bishop of Rome: all listening to each other, and all listening to the Holy Spirit, the "Spirit of Truth" (Jn 14:17), in order to know what he "says to the Churches" (Rv 2:7).'

Francis goes on to locate more precisely the role of bishop of Rome and other bishops within this vision of Church in which 'as in an inverted pyramid, the summit is located below the base'. The bishop of Rome serves the unity of the Church, is there to strengthen his brothers in the faith (Lk 22:32), while his fellow bishops are also 'vicars of Christ' by serving those over whom they have authority – the only authority is the authority of service, and 'the only power is the power of the Cross'. His insistent recall that biblical authority rests not in power for its own sake but in service is at the root of his persistent critique of clericalism and careerism in other contexts.

This is a vision of *communio* and synodality which Francis wants to see at all levels, a culture which requires structural and institutional form to make it effective. At the primary, local level he urges effective synodality through occasions of listening and sharing, with appropriate institutional form (for example, diocesan synods, councils of priests, pastoral councils), in touch 'with those on the ground', the base.

At the secondary, intermediate level, of provinces and regions, local councils and episcopal conferences, he notes that 'in a synodal Church it is not appropriate for the Pope to replace the local Episcopates in the discernment of all the problems that present themselves in their territories'. He goes to say that '… In this sense I am conscious of the need to promote a healthy "decentralisation".'

At the third, universal level, Francis wants the Synod of Bishops to become a real expression of episcopal collegiality, effective as well as affective, so that there also occurs that 'conversion of the papacy', which John Paul II had already hinted at in his 1995 appeal for help (also among ecumenical partners), in re-envisaging the Petrine ministry (see also EG, 16 and 32). Francis is clear indeed that this notion of a synodal Church 'has significant ecumenical implications'.

This Address of Francis – drawing on many of the themes already articulated in *Evangelii Gaudium,* and in his first major interview to the Jesuit magazines – indicates with crystal clarity what his vision of Church is and what strategic means are required to realise the vision. This is no mere 'intuitive' whim, some accidental novelty. Rather, Francis is recalling the Church to its biblical, first millennium and Second Vatican Council roots (he quotes the words of John Chrysostom that 'church and synod are synonymous'), he is affirming that synodality is 'a constitutive element of the Church', daring to hope that a synodal Church can become 'a banner among the nations' in mirroring the participation, solidarity and transparency that can serve as a real inspiration for governments and civil society.

The two-phase Synod of Bishops on the Family was the first

major test of the strategic implementation of this vision: the prior consultation among all the faithful, the invitation to bishops to take responsibility in the context of frank and open dialogue, the attempt to create a space for discernment and the pre-eminent role of the Holy Spirit. And the fact that it succeeded, despite all the imperfections (Francis himself noted in his address that synodality 'is an easy concept to put into words, not so easy to put into practice'), is a major step forward along the path of synodality.

This path offers a different model of Church from that operative over so many recent centuries – and in this context one recalls again the work of Avery Dulles on different models of the Church (1974), drawing inspiration from the philosopher of science Thomas Kuhn with his notion of 'paradigm shifts' (1962). Rush, in his analysis of the 'inverted pyramid' of Francis puts it this way: 'When compared with the dominant self-understanding characterising the church across the whole of the second millennium, the change constitutes nothing less than a reconfiguration of the Catholic imagination regarding the nature of the church'.[114] It is, however, a model with deep roots in the Christian tradition, and in this sense the 'revolution' of Francis is entirely traditional, albeit with suitable modifications to acknowledge the distinctiveness of our globalised world and the values, despite the downsides, of the very different, more centralised ecclesial model of the last millennium.

Cardinal Kasper has called this a 'programme for a century or more'.[115] In it Francis roots his notion of synodality explicitly in the Second Vatican Council notion of the share of all the baptised in the priestly and prophetic (teaching) roles of Jesus Christ, and implicitly (in speaking of all having a say) in the kingly (governing) role (see EG, 102–4, for explicit mention of the decision making role of laity, including women). I think in this context that the more reactionary conservatives are correct in sensing that by initiating processes rather than aiming immediately for concrete results (EG, 223) Francis is on course to change the Church more radically and lastingly. When a place is created for the voice of the peripheries to

114 Rush, op. cit., 307.
115 *National Catholic Reporter,* 20 October 2014.

be heard (the poor, women, those ill at ease with the current Church positions on sexuality and gender), then a dynamic for change is created that is hard to resist. We will examine later the legitimate fears and real obstacles that such an approach entails, and of how Francis is hopeful that the notion of discernment can help to resolve seemingly intractable stand-offs.

In the meantime – as Bishop Bonny of Antwerp noted in his assessment that the time was not right in the recent synod to peacefully go any further on the issue of homosexuality – we need to recall that prudence and patience, as well as courage and risk-taking, are Christian virtues. We need as well to be respectful of the diversity of opinion in the Church, and yet honest in advancing viewpoints, always in a spirit which seeks to preserve the unity willed by God, whose Holy Spirit personifies unity in diversity. One recalls the maxim sometimes ascribed to St Augustine: *In necessariis unitas, in dubiis libertas, in omnibus caritas* (in essentials, unity; in contested matters, freedom; in everything, charity).

Relevance of the synodal model: why does it matter?
I have several times claimed that this synodal model of Church is of crucial importance in our contemporary world. How can this claim be justified?

It is worth recalling that for Francis any talk of structural reform and ecclesial models only makes sense in the context of a missionary conversion grounded in our faith encounter with Jesus Christ. So, he can say that '... the structural and organisational reforms are secondary ... the first reform must be the attitude' (Interview), '... without new life and an authentic evangelical spirit ... any new structures will soon prove ineffective' (EG, 26), and, most clearly of all, in words to the coordinating committee of CELAM, 'the "change of structures" (from obsolete to new ones) will not be the result of reviewing an organisational flow chart, which would lead to static reorganisation; rather it will result from the very dynamics of mission. What makes obsolete structures pass away, what leads to a change of heart in Christians, is precisely a missionary spirit'.[116]

116 R. Gaillardetz, *National Catholic Reporter*, 25 September 2013.

At the same time, it is also clear that for him – and perhaps he learned this from the failures of implementation after the Second Vatican Council – structural, cultural, legal and institutional reform are essential accompaniments of missionary conversion. Indeed there is reciprocity of cause and effect at work here: mission leads to reform, and reform facilitates and empowers mission (see EG, 19–49). What I want to re-emphasise here is that what is involved is not simply a matter of organisational tidiness, but has to do with faith, with theology, with spirituality – it is part of the logic of the Incarnation that the personal and interpersonal are primary, but that they thrive only when there is appropriate institutional support.

Irish Jesuit David Harold-Barry, who has spent most of his life as a missionary in Africa, brings this out well when he asks us to focus more 'on the spiritual texture of the present malaise', in the Irish context.[117] He asks to go beyond exhaustive descriptions of our crisis to ask the question: Where is God in all this? He suggests – drawing on Ignatius of Loyola and John of the Cross (imprisoned for a time in Toledo) – that while the Church in Ireland is in desolation, in a 'dark night', desolation (when we feel 'harassed by anxiety, afflicted with sadness and face all sorts of obstacles') may be part of God's providential way of nudging us to accept change, and the dark night can be a time of 'sheer grace', 'the place of encounter' with God, the God who loves us to death (*ti amo da morire*). He goes on to urge the Church towards a new encounter – with itself, with society and with God, and encourages us in so doing to stop speaking tired language about God and begin to share our actual experience of God.

In a somewhat similar vein, speaking from a North American context but with wider application, Bradford Hinze suggests a link between desolation and his positive notion of lamentation as a call of the Spirit, sensitive to the aspirations of those who suffer. He goes on – beyond the conventional interpretation of desolation in the Spiritual Exercises of St Ignatius – to suggest that '... could it be that occasionally, not always, a believer, and by extension a

---

117 David Harold-Barry SJ, 'A Toledo Dungeon – Is the Irish Church in a "Dark Night"?', *The Furrow*, 68, December 2017, 668–72, at 668.

community, might be in desolation, consonant with what we have identified as lamentation not only because of sin and temptation, or solely because of one's radical poverty and dependency, but because of the agency of God advancing an unfinished work and a new stage of development?'[118]

I think what Francis is spelling out is that the new encounter, which Harold-Barry recommends, and the new stage of development, which Hinze points to, are best realised in a synodal Church. In his own Address Francis alludes to the reasons for this in a general way: this path is necessary because '... the world ... demands that the Church strengthens cooperation in all areas of her mission' (Address). We need to examine a little more closely why this is so.

I think, first, at a fairly obvious level, Francis is referring to the fact that when subsidiarity is exercised in a synodal model of Church, then local churches are stronger in taking responsibility for the signs of the times in their own regions and are likely to be more effective. We saw, for example, that in Ireland the bishops were, understandably, some way ahead of where Rome was on the matter of clerical child sexual abuse and its reporting to civil authorities at the turn of the millennium, and yet felt the temptation at least to defer to Roman leadership.[119] Francis is hoping to encourage more self-reliance in our diverse and pluralistic world (as, again, in the example of the papal referral of the possibility of married priests in the Amazonian region, raised by local bishop Erwin Krautler, to a regional synod in the first instance, and the translation of liturgical texts at local and regional levels), without damaging universal communion.

At a deeper level, however, I think what Francis understands is that in so many places in our world – including Ireland – the surrounding secular and civic culture is inimical to the more institutional, centralised and authoritarian mode of organisation and governance that had become characteristic of the Catholic Church even in the post-conciliar period. What is valued today is an alternative order, a new 'social imaginary', that is more horizontal, egalitarian,

---

118 Hinze, op. cit., 2016, 87.
119 Gerry O'Hanlon, 'Submission to the Australian Royal Commission Into Institutional Responses to Child Sexual Abuse', *Doctrine and Life*, 67, March 2017, 53–64.

discourse based, with enormous appreciation for the human person, experience, story and authenticity, and not least for those previously considered insignificant. These aspects of contemporary culture are entirely compatible with the gospel message, and in this context a practice of consultation, inclusion and the sharing of experience is a 'much more culturally appropriate constellation'[120] for the Church to adopt if it wants to 'attract', to discover a new language with which to communicate so that its voice may be heard.

It is sometimes objected that the Church should be counter-cultural and not simply adapt to the passing whims of fashion. The late Michael Paul Gallagher often used the phrase 'cultural discernment'.[121] Jesus was Jewish and adapted his message to the Hebrew idiom and culture, while being free to challenge it in a very radical way. Similarly, St Paul was able to take on the Gentile world on its own stage of the Athenian *Areopagus*, without losing the specificity of the gospel. And throughout the early period of the Church – think of the Apologists, the use by the Church Fathers and Mothers of the Greco-Roman heritage – on into the medieval world and later, it was ever thus, and rightly so: the Word became Flesh, we are of necessity historical beings. And yet, of course, the objections have a point: it is easy to be seduced into a too comfortable alliance with 'the world' so that the salt does indeed lose its flavour and we are no longer operating under the sign of the Cross, as plenty of historical examples show. This, in Gallagher's view, is the point of discernment.

In our present context we have already indicated a certain compatibility between a synodal way of being Church and some good points in post-modern culture. However, we have also noted divergences. As mentioned, the excessive focus on the individual has resulted in a loss of a sense of the common good, and a culture of consumerism that is driven by a neo-liberal economic model so hegemonic that is has shifted from being a framework for economic policy alone to a comprehensive grounding for political rationality. The resulting inequality and 'globalisation of indifference' are

120 Conway, op. cit.
121 Michael Paul Gallagher SJ, *Clashing Symbols, An Introduction to Faith and Culture*, London: Darton, Longman & Todd, 1997.

almost impervious to a culture which tends, in much of the western world, to relegate religion to the private sphere and to suffer from a kind of epistemological and moral relativism which, in 'post-truth' fashion, disregards evidence in favour of the already powerful.

It seems, then, that in its attempt to dialogue in a constructively critical way with the world, the Church would do well to adopt what is good in the culture, if it is consistent with its own foundation and tradition. We have indicated how a synodal Church ticks these boxes very appropriately. We are then, ironically, in a much better position to be counter-cultural and prophetic on what we have discerned as needing correction. In this sense the Church – as *Gaudium et Spes* indicated so well – both teaches and learns from the world.

Finally, with regard to the relevance of the synodal model, Massimo Faggioli notes its suitability when it comes to tackling pluralism and change within the Church itself.[122] A synodal process, as envisaged and acted on by Francis, is one which admits that there are disagreements on important issues within the Church (as there always have been) and decides to address these disagreements with a *process* that is *synodal* and is effected through *spiritual discernment*.[123] This inclusive process, with its ambition to hear all voices (the 'sense of the faithful'), to listen to experts (theologians) and to value legitimate authority (the bishops and pope) is in contrast to some tendencies within the surrounding political environment of secular democracies where there is contempt for elites and experts and a turn to populists and special interests, not to mention rising authoritarianism. This is why Francis in his address dared to hope that new way of being Church might become a 'banner among the nations' and Faggioli echoes this hope in the context of current political difficulties: 'Handling in a synodal way the issue of pluralism within the church is important for the church ... but is important also for our world that looks at the church with a glimpse of hope, trying to see if in dealing with this universe of diversities Christians can succeed where others are failing.'[124]

---

122 Massimo Faggioli, *Catholicism and Citizenship, Political Cultures of the Church in the Twenty-First Century,* Collegeville, MN: Liturgical Press, 2017, especially chapter 3.
123 Ibid., 65.
124 Ibid., 66.

Will Francis succeed?
I have already outlined some of Francis's successes to date in his desire to undertake a missionary reform of the Church, as well as the ongoing opposition to his project. Improvements to the oversight of Vatican finances and to procedures around clerical child sexual abuse, the promotion of women to posts of responsibility, the gradual reorganisation of the Curia towards greater service of the universal Church with some change of personnel and a calling out of clericalism, the appointment of new bishops and cardinals – all these and more are concrete instances of Church reform. I have also argued that at the heart of his reform is the synodal process, a different way of being Church, within which all these particular instances of reform are embedded, and out of which they arise. But Francis, as he knows well himself, is old, his papacy will not be a long one. He is trying to bring about a revolution in an institution which has a long memory and deep cultural habits. Will it take root, will it last?

The importance of the cultural factor should not be underestimated. Organisational theorists have known for a long time that vision (mission) and strategy are not sufficient for group reform. As with all clichés, the slogan (attributed to organisational theorist Peter Drucker) 'culture eats strategy for breakfast' contains some truth.[125] Apart from outright and stiff resistance, there is also present at many levels in the Church at the moment (not just in curial Rome) a kind of unconscious passive aggression that results in minimal compliance with the reforms of Francis – a sense that 'this too will pass' and before too long we can get back to 'business as usual', the 'way we do things around here'. In this context it is worth referring to the saying, which Hinze recalls: 'apathy is frozen violence'.[126] This is as much a matter of a change of feeling and imagination as it is of ideas and convictions.

It is surely at least partly this reality that Francis was pointing to in

125 See Thomas von Mitschke-Collande, 'Fit for Purpose', *The Tablet*, 14 September 2013, 13–16; Robert H. Waterman Jr, Thomas J. Peters and Julien R. Philips, 'Structure if not Organisation', *Business Horizons*, June 1980; Eddy Molloy, 'Public Service Reform, The Central Importance of Character and Culture', Magill Summer School, 2013.
126 Hinze, op. cit., 2016, 59.

his closing speech at the Synod of Bishops in October 2015 when he spoke frankly about the unveiling of closed hearts, the expression of opinions in not entirely well-meaning ways, and the unwelcome preference for the letter over the spirit. There will, of course, be some bishops who are so opposed to change that they will remain deaf to the invitation to travel in a new direction. And the media, which thrives on conflict and crisis, will always, at least in the short term, tend to frame the story in terms of possible schism and heresy, even when the evidence points to overwhelming support for Francis.

Many bishops in particular – including those who regard themselves as middle-ground conservatives – may well (as happened at the Second Vatican Council) discover that having a voice at a synod, getting to know others in small groups, being freer from the previous 'command and control' model is something that they like and is liberating. There are small signs – also in Ireland – that bishops and local conferences are beginning to become aware of the new freedom and responsibility they have been given. They are likely to warm to the invitation from Francis to learn more positive dispositions for discernment[127] – not by simply abandoning cherished convictions, but by allowing themselves to acknowledge that others, with different convictions, are also part of the one group and that we need to find a way of moving forward together. Something like this seems to have happened in the German language group during the synod itself, with profound effects on the rest of the assembly, since it had seemed from previous utterances that the positions of Cardinals Kasper and Mueller were simply irreconcilable.

This again is where patience is needed – the Catholic Church has a lot of catching up to do in learning 'best practice' in terms of a more participative way of proceeding, but it will only learn by trying. And this needs to happen at local level too, so that participants at the Synod of Bishops become well used to the cut and thrust of debate. This will require formation over generations and will not happen overnight. However, it can begin overnight, and immediately: we need to learn by doing, beginning at parish and parish council level,

---

127 Gerry O'Hanlon, 'Discernment and the Synod on the Family', *Doctrine and Life,* 65, September 2015, 9–20.

with diocesan assemblies and synods becoming regular and not just rare events.

We also need the humility to acknowledge that we can learn from others – from Churches, like the Orthodox and other Christian Churches, with their long traditions of synodality; and from secular experts with good skills in group facilitation – always in a context where we also learn the new skill of combining the collegial aspects of synodality with the primatial, which is proper to the Catholic tradition.

Conclusion

The jury is still out as to whether Francis can succeed in realising this new model of Church. It depends on change at so many levels – personal and cultural, structural, legal and institutional. But change has begun to happen and, as Vatican commentator Joshua McElwee observes: 'Transformation builds slowly as a culture shifts'.[128]

One thing is clear: if Francis is to succeed then it cannot be without the active support of bishops worldwide. It is true that the pope is particularly popular among laity worldwide and 'it is difficult to image a successor changing the direction of such a popular pope – at least not openly – without causing a schism in the Catholic Church',[129] but it would be entirely counter-intuitive and, indeed, counter-productive to build synodal reform on a kind of 'papolatry'. The popularity and moral authority of the current pope can exercise a crucial leadership function in this revolutionary change, but without buy-in from local and regional hierarchies an indispensable dimension is missing. The People of God as a whole are clearly ready for change: but they require their leadership to come on board also if this is truly to be an ecclesial happening, and not simply an extra-institutional, congregationalist type change that would not be true to the nature of the Catholic Church. This will not be easy for bishops, for whom the cultural and other challenges are significant: but called to the difficult role of leadership, of Good Shepherd, in challenging times, they will perhaps recognise that embracing this

128 Joshua J. McElwee, *National Catholic Reporter*, 9 March 2017.
129 Isabelle de Gaulmyn, 'Will Pope Francis' Reforms Last?', *La Croix*, 1 June 2017.

synodal turn is their best chance of transforming the current crisis into a real opportunity.

Of course – to return to basics once again – in Christian understanding it is God, the Holy Spirit, who is the principal actor in this drama which has so many indispensable accompanying roles, including those of bishops and all the faithful. Typically the early stages of encounter with God – as in any love story – are redolent of a beauty and tenderness that easily attract, the glory of God that von Balthasar speaks of, a form that captivates and enraptures, takes us out of ourselves, leads to joyous mission. However, as our journey through life progresses, we become aware that the 'glory of the Lord shall be revealed' (Is 40:5) as a beauty which integrates suffering, illness, what seems like ugliness (the Suffering Servant), evil and even death – this is the God of Power who empties self (Ph 2:5–11), becoming like us in all things, even unto death itself. And this means entering into deeper levels of our encounter with God, into the mystery of suffering and the purifying silence of God, the encounter with the Cross. Church reform will go through all these stages too, led by the Holy Spirit, and will also always be shot through with the hope of Resurrection, the confidence that comes from God's promise that love is stronger than all else.

If one understands Charles Taylor's category of 'social imaginary' as a way of envisioning the world that captures attention, engages life passions and addresses laments,[130] then I have been arguing that the People of God as synodal Church in constructively critical dialogue with our world, proposed by Pope Francis, is an ecclesial social imaginary that addresses the signs of our times.

However, I have also noted that some legitimate questions remain as to whether this can really be so in practice. In particular, will it not lead to the kind of doctrinal development that signifies a rupture with the past, as many fear? Will it not introduce a polarisation and fragmentation into the Catholic Church, which a more democratic form of leadership is less able to contain than the previously more unified, monarchical mode of governance? After all, we have been recently commemorating the Protestant Reformation, and, despite

130 See Hinze, op. cit., 2016, 190–92

its many blessings, are newly aware of the long-lasting effects of polarisation. Orthodox and Protestant Churches alike have their own problems around synodality, which is clearly no silver bullet for all problems of ecclesial flourishing. The attempt to combine unity and diversity is not simple to realise in human affairs, and the temptation to retreat to a unity based on uniformity is always there. Part Three looks a more considered treatment of these inter-related issues around teaching and governance.

PART THREE

Emerging Issues:
Teaching and Governance

CHAPTER FIVE

Teaching in a Synodal Church

*Rejoice always ... do not quench the Spirit, do not despise
prophesying, but test everything ... He who calls you is faithful.*
(1 Th 16–24)

One of the critical stumbling blocks along the way towards the
creation of a synodal Church is mutual incomprehension around
questions of truth and Church teaching. When some Catholics
persistently question official Church doctrine on various issues,
others ask why can they not simply obey, or, if that's not possible,
why don't they join another Christian community more congenial
to their beliefs? Both sides, we may assume, are sincere. How may
we live together in one Church? Must one side simply cede to the
other?

To come at this more concretely and, in the light of the recent papal
document on marriage *Amoris Laetitia*, more existentially – is not
adultery always simply wrong, against God's commandments, and is
not any attempt to 'water this down', as in (contrary to the teaching
of John Paul II and previous popes) permitting Catholics in second
unions access to the Eucharist under certain conditions, either a
false change of doctrine or a mistaken pastoral application of mercy
to a binding teaching of the Church?[131] Can we not be certain about
Church teaching, especially when successive popes have taught the
same, and does this not make the present pope's apparent deviation
from 'traditional' teaching suspect? After all, don't people die for
the faith, for truth, and haven't many contemporary Catholics made
considerable and generous sacrifices in obedience to teaching that

131 Gerry O'Hanlon, 'The Joy of Love – *Amoris Laetitia*', *The Furrow*, 67, June 2016, 328–36.

the world may not understand and which other Catholics contest (one thinks, for example, about teaching on contraception and the ordination of women to priesthood)?

And yet ... we have also seen how significantly the Church has changed its position and teaching vis-à-vis dialogue with the world and its own internal constitution from the time of the 'long nineteenth century' to the Second Vatican Council and since. To this could be added so many other changes to what had seemed like unalterable Church teaching over many decades and centuries – teaching on slavery, on usury, on religious freedom, on the inferiority of women and the headship of man in marriage, to name but a few of many such changes. Does it not become increasingly embarrassing and lacking in credibility to deny that change can occur? Is this not something that, rightly, our contemporary culture, with its admittedly sometimes extreme esteem for 'authenticity', rejects?

We have noted the fears that a synodal Church is being introduced as a kind of Trojan horse, a 'jesuitical' ploy, to introduce doctrinal change over the longer term, allegedly part of the current pope's agenda of 'playing a long game' (despite his own appearance of doctrinal conservatism). We have noted too the real downside of polarisation within and between Christian communities on issues of truth, so that it is clear that some criteria of fidelity to truth are desirable for individuals and the community as a whole. 'Who do you say that I am?' (Mk 8:29) We need to be able to answer such questions if our relationship with God is really what matters, what we live and die for, if we are to be able 'to give an account of the hope that is within us' (1 Pt 3:15) in a post-modern age which is careless and cynical about the possibility and even desirability of objective truth. But how to combine respect for truth's objectivity with its historicity? And how, within a synodal context, to give due weight to the 'sense of the faithful' without confusing it with constantly changing public opinion? Can a synodal Church, rather than being an obstacle, become a help towards reconciling the deeply held polarities around this issue?

I want to propose some lines of approach to this crucial matter.

À la carte Catholicism? The question of truth

It will be a help to recall that theologically questions of truth and teaching are understood within a differentiated and sophisticated framework that challenges any simplistic account.[132] As the Second Vatican Council taught in *Unitatis Redintegratio*, there is a hierarchy of truths (UR, 11), so that some (for example, the Resurrection) are more foundational to our faith than others (for example, the existence and role of angels). This objective hierarchy of truths was reinforced in the theology of Karl Rahner by the notion of a subjective or 'existential' hierarchy, according to which the faithful might choose to exercise a legitimate non-emphasis, 'a failing to notice' at least for a time, with respect to certain less fundamental truths that they experience as burdensome and cannot for the moment accept with integrity.[133] This latter approach combines well an esteem for conscience and personal authenticity with respect for the normative nature of God's word and of the wider tradition to which one belongs.

There are also degrees of certainty with which truths are proposed for our acceptance. Formerly this was treated under the rubric of 'theological notes',[134] by which a particular grade was assigned to each truth – for example, at the top end, 'defined faith', then towards the middle 'Catholic doctrine', and towards the end of the scale, the delightfully entitled 'scandalous to pious ears' (*piis auribus offensivus*). The latter points to a further refinement necessary in modern times – in the past it was possible to imagine that theologians could have a certain freedom to speculate on contentious Church teaching in the privacy of academic journals and conferences. Now, however, with the global communications revolution, there is a democratisation of information which quickly allows specialised knowledge to become accessible to all. And even if, as Gabriel Daly points out,[135] this practice of ascribing 'theological notes'

132 For what follows, see Gerry O'Hanlon, 'Irish Catholicism at a Crossroads', *Studies*, 101, winter 2012, 375–84, at 376–80.
133 D. Carroll, 'A Note on Dissent – Theological and Otherwise', *Studies*, spring, 1987, 29–41, at 32–34.
134 See International Theological Commission, *Theology Today: Perspectives, Principles and Criteria*, 8 March 2012, nn. 40–41.
135 Gabriel Daly, *The Church, Always in Need of Reform*, Dublin: Dominican Publications, 2015, chapters 1, 8 and *passim*.

became overly mechanical within a Neo-Scholasticism dedicated to an exclusively propositional, deductivist and 'deposit of faith' model of revelation later rejected by the Second Vatican Council in *Dei Verbum*, nonetheless the principle of differentiating between different grades of authority and therefore certainty within the corpus of Church teaching is abidingly sound.

In addition, theology notes the importance of 'reception' for the recognition and acceptance of authentic truth – in other words there is a 'sense of the faithful' which shares in the charism of ecclesial infallibility (LG, 12) so that there is theological weight to be given to the conscientious response of the good Catholic faithful to the truths proposed to them. This 'sense of the faithful' ought, of course, also be a source or reference point of authentic truth.[136]

A document published by the International Theological Commission in 2014, authorised by Cardinal Mueller, who was then Prefect of the Congregation of the Doctrine of the Faith, is of particular significance in outlining official teaching on the 'sense of the faith/faithful'.[137] This document, entitled *'Sensus Fidei' in the Life of the Church*, can be read in the light of the desire of Pope Francis to move towards a synodal Church.

The document describes the 'sense of the faith/faithful' in terms of a certain supernatural co-naturality with the truth of the gospel, an instinct or intuition, which belongs to the baptised individual and community. This instinct is connected with, but distinct from, objective knowledge of facts: it is best understood according to the analogy of knowledge between friends. In other words, as in *Dei Verbum*, the approach is to go deeper than propositional knowledge and to move into the realm of mystery proper to the personal, including the realm of desire and feeling.

The document outlines the biblical roots of the 'sense of the faithful' and its crucial historical role, not least as understood by Cardinal Newman in his analysis of the role of the 'simple' faithful in maintaining the orthodoxy of the teaching of the Council of Nicea in the fourth century about the divinity of Christ, when the

---

136 International Theological Commission, op. cit., nn. 33–36.
137 See Gerry O'Hanlon, 'Free Speech in the Church', *Studies,* 105, summer 2016, 199–211 (at 202–3).

bishops were wavering. While it is made clear that an authentic discernment[138] of this 'sense of the faith' at any particular time and in relation to any particular issue is more than a mere survey or poll of public opinion – indeed it may not even coincide with majority public opinion, since often the truth is to be found in minority opinion – nonetheless 'public opinion is a prime means by which, in a normal way, the *sensus fidelium* can be gauged' (DV, 125). Other means are also identified – the liturgy, popular religiosity, the poor and also 'various institutional instruments by which the faithful may more formally be heard and consulted ... such as particular councils ... diocesan synods ... the pastoral council of each diocese ... and pastoral councils in parishes' (DV, 125), all involving the lay faithful.

The document goes on[139] to note that while the Magisterium is the normative interpreter of the sense of the faith, which may take considerable time to discern, where there is resistance or even rejection by the faithful to particular teaching, there is an onus on the Magisterium to consider whether the teaching needs clarification or reformulation (DV, 80), or indeed whether this may indicate that 'certain decisions have been taken by those in authority without due consideration of the experience and *sensus fidei* of the faithful, or without sufficient consultation of the faithful by the magisterium' (DV, 123). The document also notes the contribution of theology to this process, not least in exploring the various criteria of authentic discernment.

The crucial importance of the 'sense of the faith' as a source and a critical confirmation of authentic teaching is asserted, thus broadening the nineteenth-century limitation of the term 'Magisterium' (to bishops, pope and Vatican congregations only) to embrace its more historical meaning of a threefold conversation between baptised faithful, theologians and the hierarchy.[140] This is clearly the direction in which Pope Francis wants the Church to

138 See Gerry O'Hanlon, 'Discernment and the Synod on the Family', *Doctrine and Life*, 65, September 2015, 9–20.
139 See Gerry O'Hanlon, 'Where to Now? – Reflections on an Extraordinary Synod', *The Furrow*, 65, December 2014, 583–91, at 588–89.
140 See Ormond Rush, 'The Prophetic Office in the Church', in Richard R. Gaillardetz, op. cit., 89–112.

move when he speaks of a synodal Church for the future, and of a more inclusive notion of 'thinking with the church'.[141] He has illustrated how that might happen in practice by his open and consultative process throughout the recent two-phase Synod on the Family (2014–15).

What *Sensus Fidei* also makes clear is the intrinsic link between the 'sense of the faith/faithful' and an ecclesial culture which values free speech and public opinion. Interestingly, in the pre-conciliar Church, Karl Rahner, himself intermittently under a cloud from the Vatican from 1951 to 1962 (on the eve of the council), bravely wrote a significant piece in 1953 (published in English in 1959).[142] In it he referred to Pius XII's observation (1950) that 'something would be lacking in [the Church's] life if she had no public opinion. Both pastors of souls and lay people would be to blame for this', and developed his own argument for free speech in the Church.

Rahner wanted the faithful to be brought up in a responsible spirit of obedience which would make use 'of their right to express their opinions',[143] to have a 'proper critical spirit towards Church matters',[144] learning to unite 'the inevitable detachment of a critical public attitude with genuine and inspired love of the Church and a genuine subordination and submission to the actual official representatives of the Church'.[145] He went on to say that we must learn 'that even in the Church there can be a body something like Her Majesty's Opposition, which in the course of Church history has always had its own kind of saints in its ranks – the ranks of a genuine, divinely willed opposition to all that is merely human in the Church and her official representatives'.[146] He argued that not only do the faithful have a right to speak out in certain circumstances, but also a duty.[147]

In the context of the political culture of his time, current and recent

141 See Gerry O'Hanlon, 'The Quiet Revolution – Reflections on Synod 2015', *The Furrow*, 66, December 2015, 632–41.
142 Karl Rahner, *Free Speech in the Church*, New York, NY: Sheed and Ward, 1959; see Gerry O'Hanlon, *Free Speech in the Church*, op. cit., 199–200.
143 Ibid., 36.
144 Ibid., loc. cit.
145 Ibid., loc. cit.
146 Ibid., 36–37.
147 Ibid., 37.

(Communism, Nazism and Fascism in Europe), Rahner cautioned that 'the Church today should be more careful than ever before not to give even the slightest impression that she is of the same order as those totalitarian states for whom outward power and sterile obedience are everything and love and freedom are nothing, and that her methods of government are those of the totalitarian systems in which public opinion has become a Ministry of Propaganda'.[148] And, with admirable restraint and delicacy, he noted that even today 'we – both those of us who are in authority and those who are under authority – are perhaps still accustomed here and there to certain patriarchal forms of leadership and obedience which have no essential or lasting connection with the real stuff of Church authority and obedience'.[149]

Some Implications of a synodal approach to truth
The Second Vatican Council made it clear that the 'sense of the faith' is linked to the share of the baptised in the office of Jesus Christ as prophet, and a synodal reading of this opens out into the threefold conversation between hierarchy, theologians and sense of the faithful, with the differentiated functions already described.

Commentators have warned that, given what we know of his past, Pope Francis is unlikely to suddenly change Church positions on so-called neuralgic issues (mostly to do with sexuality and gender).[150] Irish Redemptorist Tony Flannery is interesting on this. Rather than unilaterally change any particular Church teaching, Flannery would love the new pope '… to create a climate within the Church where there is freedom of thought and expression, where issues can be discussed and debated. Because that is the only way in which to bring about real change. Change that comes from on high is no good, and will not survive. But change that comes through a process of discussion, or dialogue, as we call it in the Church, is the enduring kind of change.'[151]

It is worth unpacking a little the theological presuppositions

148 Ibid., 38.
149 Ibid., loc. cit.
150 For what follows, see Gerry O'Hanlon, 'Whispers of the Spirit – the Church of the Future', *The Furrow*, 64, June 2013, 332–41, at 338–40.
151 Ibid., 338.

underlying Flannery's position, in particular as it relates to Church teaching. We have been immersed in an ecclesial culture which has simplified and centralised the search for truth in a reductive way.[152] In particular we have tended to magnify the role of the Vatican and papal magisterium, and reduce that of theologians and the faithful, not to mention that of bishops other than the pope.

In this context Richard Gaillardetz[153] notes that the need to consult the faithful makes sense not primarily as some exercise in liberal democracy but more essentially because of the theological nature of the Church, in which the Holy Spirit also acts through the sharing of the faithful in the prophetic (teaching office) of Jesus Christ, spoken about in terms of the 'sense of the faithful' (LG, 12, 35; DV, 8). Of course, it is not always easy to determine the exact contents of the 'sense of the faithful', to establish a consensus, in particular when new issues emerge or older questions are considered in new contexts. Nonetheless the search for this consensus is important since it is a consensus that shares in the charism of infallibility (LG, 12).

None of this contests the role of bishops, including the pope, as authoritative guardians of faith and teachers of truth. But it does draw attention to their mandate not to teach new revelation, but only what has been passed on – and a principal source of what needs to be passed on is precisely what the faithful believe. Cardinal Newman, author of *On Consulting the Faithful in Matters of Doctrine* (1859), speaks of this in terms of the '*conspiratio fidelium et pastorum*' – the 'breathing together of the faithful and pastors'. In this '*conspiratio*' bishops, far from being pitted against laity, are in fact understood to be part of the 'faithful', the whole Church both teaches and learns, and bishops in particular, along with careful and prayerful study of Scripture and Tradition, need also to inquire after the insights of the faithful as part of their teaching exercise. The bishop – including of course the bishop of Rome – is then both teacher and learner. The third-century bishop St Cyprian

152 O'Hanlon, 'The People of God: Towards a Renewed Church?' in Suzanne Mulligan (ed.), *Reaping the Harvest: Fifty Years after Vatican* II, Dublin: Columba Press, 2012, 63–87, at 70–75.
153 Gaillardetz, 2003, op. cit., 107–20.

of Carthage, who made free use of consultation in the exercise of his episcopal office, expresses this well:

But it is unrepentant presumption and insolence that induces men to defend their own perverse errors instead of giving assent to what is right and true, but has come from another. The blessed apostle Paul foresaw this when he wrote to Timothy with the admonition that a bishop should not be wrangling or quarrelsome but gentle and teachable. Now a man is teachable if he is meek and gentle and patient in learning. It is a bishop's duty not only to teach but also to learn. For he becomes a better teacher if he makes daily progress and advancement in learning what is better.[154]

Australian theologian Ormond Rush develops a similar approach.[155] He proposes a synthesis in which the one teaching office of the Church (sharing in the prophetic office of Jesus Christ) has three distinct authorities: the sense of the faithful, theology and the Magisterium[156] (LG, 12, 25; DV 8). The authority of the magisterium is distinct precisely through its authoritative formal judgement and official formulation of Church teaching – but the lay faithful in particular, through their interpretative sense of the faith as they apply the gospel to daily life, must be allowed to contribute to this formal process. Their 'sense of the faith' is a privileged expression of the lived faith of the whole Church, and in his more recent reflection on this issue Rush believes that Pope Francis is making moves to resolve the tension in the Second Vatican Council between the infallibility of the 'sense of the faith' in believing and the infallibility of papal teaching in teaching. He is doing so, according to Rush, by pointing towards a synthesis with his notion of a synodal Church, in which 'the linchpin linking the two infallibilities is listening to the *sensus fidelium'*, so that '... the *sensus fidelium,* and listening to the *sensus fidelium,* lies at the heart of Francis's dynamic notion of a synodal Church'.[157]

154 Gaillardetz, 2003, op. cit., 112.
155 Ormond Rush, 'The Prophetic Office in the Church', in R. Gaillerdetz (ed.), 2012, op. cit., 89–112.
156 Ibid., 96.
157 Oromond Rush, 'Inverting the Pyramid: The *Sensus Fidelium* in a Synodal Church', *Theological Studies,* 78, June 2017, 299–325, at 311–12.

Similarly, the Magisterium is dependent on the scholarly expertise of theologians with respect to faithful interpretation of Scripture and Tradition within new contexts.[158] Both faithful and theologians are necessary to this process because the Magisterium can only teach what is the faith of the Church, under the authority of Scripture and Tradition.

Ormond goes on to note that it is the same Holy Spirit who assists all three authorities in the one teaching office, noting that the early Church came to recognise that this '*conspiratio*' of the Holy Spirit with the faithful, theologians and Magisterium was best respected and attended to by the instrument of council or synod, in dialogue (Acts 15:28: 'it has seemed good to the Holy Spirit and to us' – the Council of Jerusalem concerning the major issue of the Gentiles).

Of course it makes good epistemological sense to make the case that the search for truth is best undertaken together, within a culture of 'merry debate' and cheerful disputation',[159] that it is short-sighted to presume that any authorities on their own, much less a single authority, simply 'know best'. But here I am locating this epistemology within a theological reading of Church and its responsibility to and for truth. We have been living with a reductive sense of Magisterium, and, in particular, its effective limitation to a centralised form which too often tends towards Congar's critique of a 'creeping infallibility'. A more inclusive notion of Church teaching would respect the need for appropriate structures of consultation – such as inclusive synods and/or councils – and encourage a culture of dialogue along the lines that many in the Church have long called for. We could hope that, over time, in such a renewed and reformed Church ecclesial teaching, no matter how challenging, might have a better chance of more widespread and peaceful reception.

158 And so, for example, it sounded strange when Pope Benedict, in a valedictory address to priests, claimed that many important aspects of the interpretation of the Second Vatican Council which prevailed immediately after the council were simply media-driven (see Sandro Magister, www.chiesa.espressonline.it, 15 February 2013), when in fact they have perfectly legitimate theological credentials (see Massimo Faggioli, *Vatican II, The Battle for Meaning*, New York, NY: Paulist Press, 2012), not to mention grounding in the 'sense of the faithful'. For an interesting account of the link between a restorationist hermeneutic of the Second Vatican Council and the 'Communio project', see Gerard Mannion, 'Magisterium as a Social Imaginary', in Gaillardetz (ed.), 2012, op. cit., 113–39.

159 Ladislas Orsy, 'Fifty Years later: the Council lives', *Doctrine and Life*, 62, October 2012, 5–11, at 8–9.

Nonetheless, we also know that truth, and, in particular, certainty about truth, is elusive. Disputes about truth will always be a characteristic of a pilgrim Church – we need to sustain ourselves by a theology and spirituality which respect this reality in a constructive way and preserve unity, an essential mark of a Church that claims to be universal and catholic. A Swedish Jesuit, Fredrick Heiding, draws on the writings of Karl Rahner to offer a perspective which may be of interest, not least given Pope Francis's Jesuit and Ignatian background.[160]

Having established the theological grounds for legitimate disagreement, Rahner offers seven pointers to appropriate attitudes and dispositions in matters of dissent – love for the Church (in the concrete, warts and all, including a respect and even affection of office-holders); a humble attitude, which does not take oneself too seriously, a lack of excessive self-importance; criticism may be legitimate, but it must not be characterised as 'giving carte blanche to an unrestrained desire for criticism and an unbridled wanting-to-know-everything-better';[161] some theological knowledge; serious engagement with the Church teaching in question, serious effort to appreciate and assimilate it positively, to overcome one's own lack of sympathy; a cheerful attitude of good will, so that 'he or she is able to laugh and is after all attached to the criticised men of the Church in loving benevolence – when he or she knows that even though they are not geniuses nor saints, but at a closer look they turn out just as lovable, well-disposed and sensible as one believes oneself to be';[162] finally, one should not express criticism in such a way that it sounds as if one is standing outside the Church community. This will involve a real empowerment of those in the Church now suffering from an unequal distribution of power.

Perhaps Rahner's approach, challenging as it is, may best be summed up in a presupposition expressed by Ignatius towards the start of his Spiritual Exercises: '... it is necessary to suppose that every good Christian is more ready to put a good interpretation on

160 Frederik Heiding SJ, *Ignatian Spirituality at Ecclesial Frontiers,* Oxford: 2012, 198–219, especially 212–15.
161 Ibid., 213.
162 Ibid., 214.

another's statement than to condemn it as false' (Sp. Ex., 22). The challenge of course is to foster a culture of dialogue in our Church, which allows for conflict, but learns to conduct it in a loving way – as the biblical template proposes, with its call for both personal conversion and appropriate institutional and structural embodiment.

Pastoral Theology separate from Doctrinal and Moral?
It is sometimes suggested that pastoral theology, involving the merciful application of unchanging principles, can develop and change in a way that doctrine and morality cannot. In other words, as with those who seek to reduce the significance of the Second Vatican Council because of its predominantly 'pastoral' nature argue (despite the two dogmatic constitutions and the clear doctrinal and moral content of other decrees), while change may be possible with respect to ecclesial discipline and pastoral application, it is contended that the basic truths of the Church about doctrine and morality must always remain the same.

This point of view may explain the curious reality at the Synod on the Family[163] that the vast majority of participants (and external commentators) expressed views similar to those attributed to Cardinal Oswald Gracias (co-drafter of the final synod document and member of the pope's standing C-9 Council) that 'theology and church discipline can develop, though doctrine remains the same'.[164] This is curious, because from scriptural times onwards our Church has acknowledged doctrinal development – think, within Scripture and in the context of a discussion on marriage, of the exceptive clause about the prohibition of divorce in Matthew, the Pauline privilege, and later, by means of Church authority, the Petrine privilege;[165] think of the far more radical development of doctrine, within scriptural times, of the inclusion of the Gentiles; of the early

---

163 For what follows, see Gerry O'Hanlon, 'The Quiet Revolution – Reflections on Synod 2015', *The Furrow*, 66, December 2015, 632–41, at 637–39; and 'Where to Now? Reflections on an Extraordinary Synod', *The Furrow*, 65, December 2014, 583–91.
164 *The Tablet*, 31 October 2015, 6.
165 Bishop Bonny puts it this way in his pre-synodal remarks before the first synod's first phase: 'In short: the teaching of the Catholic Church on marriage and family is to be found in a broad tradition that has acquired new form and new content down through the centuries', *The Furrow*, 65, October 2014, 456.

Christological and Trinitarian debates and the crucial doctrinal development involved; of the universally acknowledged work by Cardinal Newman, *An Essay on The Development of Christian Doctrine* (1845); of recent documents from the International Theological Commission.[166]

Of course there is a serious concern underling the synod's insistence that what was at stake was a matter of discipline or pastoral application and practice, and not doctrine. This concern lies in unresolved problems within our Church about the more precise nature of development – is it always a matter of elucidating and more clearly drawing out truths which are already implicitly contained in prior formulations (echoed in Joseph Ratzinger's distinction, in speaking about true reform,[167] between 'principles' which remain the same and 'concrete historical situations and their demands' which lead to a certain necessary discontinuity)? Or are there occasions where development is more dialectical and corrective (think, as mentioned before, of the doctrine on slavery, the relatively uncontroverted change that has occurred within the last century concerning the doctrine of the headship of the man in marriage,[168] the 'counter-syllabus' referred to by Ratzinger himself in speaking about the corrections that key decrees of the Second Vatican Council – he instances *Gaudium et Spes, Dignitatis Humanae* and *Nostra Aetate* in particular – made to the *Syllabus* of Pius IX, which had so deeply affected the Catholic imagination and the relationship between Church and world)?

Theologian Edward Hahnenberg develops this line of thought through a consideration of the post-conciliar theology of ministry.[169] He argues that (as before in other areas in the history of the Church) what we assume to be a kind of natural evolution is in fact

166 International Theological Commission, '*Sensus Fidei' in the Life of the Church*, 2014, and *Theology Today: Perspectives, Principles and Criteria*, 2012.
167 See Joseph A. Komonchak, 'Benedict XVI and the Interpretation of Vatican II', in Michael. J. Lacy and Francis Oakley (eds), *The Crisis of Authority in Catholic Modernity*, Oxford: Oxford University Press, 2011, 93–110, at 100–01.
168 Philip Bacq SJ, 'La relation homme-femme dans la société occidentale et la tradition de l'Église', *En Question*, 110, septembre 2014, 27–29; and 'Tradition chrétienne et évolution de la Famille', Études,mars 2014, 29–39.
169 See Gerry O'Hanlon, 'Emerging Issues in Catholic Church Reform', *Doctrine and Life*, 66, July–August 2016, 3–15, at 4–5.

experienced at the time as an anomaly: 'what in retrospect appears as development was, at the time, experienced as disruption',[170] and the anomaly in question becomes a 'major impetus for the development of doctrine', such that the mainstream theological tradition does not simply reject prior theory but 'finds ways to revise the theory in the light of the exception'.[171]

This underlying concern needs to be addressed more explicitly by theologians and historians, and it would have helped the Synod on the Family to have had more resources of this kind at its disposal. However, in the meantime, what does not suffice is taking an almost pathological, fetish-like refuge in mantras about the impossibility of doctrinal development, mantras which are simply incredible because so at odds with our foundation story, its tradition and history.

A more persuasive account of the intrinsic relationship between the pastoral and the doctrinal has been given by Redemptorist theologian Raphael Gallagher,[172] who notes the tendency to equate pastoral theology with the application of pre-existing norms. According to this account 'real' theology would deal with timeless, objective truths while pastoral (or 'soft') theology would apply these truths in a way that took kind account of human weakness and fallibility, but without affecting the original truth. Gallagher argues (as did Bishop Bonny of Antwerp before the first phase of the synod[173]) that 'a false dichotomy between immutable doctrinal theory and changing reality risks destroying the unity necessary for a coherent personal life'.[174] So, instead of simply assuming that Church teaching is always correct and that the Church has nothing to learn from the world, we must also consider that in some cases, in particular 'where there is a serious divide between 'Christian doctrine' and 'secular life', the teaching itself needs to be reconsidered. In such cases, I would add, it is not appropriate

170 Edward P. Hahnenberg, 'Learning from Experience: Attention to Anomalies in a Theology of Ministry', in Richard R. Gaillardetz and Edward P. Hahnenberg (eds), A Church with Open Doors, Collegeville, MN: Liturgical Press, 2015, 159–80, at 172.
171 Ibid., loc. cit.
172 Raphael Gallagher, 'The Synod – A Fresh Pastoral Journey', The Furrow, 67, September 2015, 439–46.
173 The Furrow, 65, October 2014, 455–56.
174 Gallagher, op. cit., 441.

simply to invoke the 'principle of gradualness' or appeal to God's mercy – these are proper pastoral responses where there is failure to behave according to doctrine that is true, not when doctrine requires development or revision.

Gallagher is suggesting here that theology does not proceed in two acts – the first focusing on theory, the second on application. Instead he proposes a pastoral theology where doctrinal principles and actual experience are co-present to each other so that doctrine 'is necessarily open to development given that the world is on the journey to the Kingdom'.[175]

This underlying issue can also be helped by a fuller acknowledgment that, as mentioned already, not all doctrine is equally authoritative (the hierarchy of truths/theological 'notes'), that, as long ago argued by Karl Rahner[176] and as now proposed by Francis, there should be greater freedom for local episcopal conferences to discern and respond to problems in their own regions, while always maintaining communion with the whole Church, and that Magisterium operates best when there is a symbiosis between the authoritative judgement of bishops (including the bishop of Rome), theologians and the sense of the faithful.

If one adds to this complex framework the requirement to be faithful to Scripture, to Tradition, to be consistent with basic human rights and the natural law, then one begins to understand why teaching and truth may not lightly be reduced to some simple 'command and obey' model. There is a need to balance the authoritative Magisterium of the college of bishops, with the pope at their head, with the mission of theologians also to teach, so that bishops and pope must listen carefully, in particular to the 'sense of the faithful', but also to the voices of theology.

Part of our problem today is that the papal and episcopal Magisterium has become inflated to such a degree that in the popular mind all episcopal, and especially papal and Vatican utterances, become identified in a undifferentiated way with 'Church teaching', to be accepted without question. Yves Congar, as noted, spoke of the

175 Ibid., 443.
176 Karl Rahner, 'Structural Change in the Church of the Future', *Theological Investigations,* Vol. 20, London: Darton Longman & Todd, 1981, 115–32.

dangers of 'creeping infallibility' and of the incredible inflation of the papal teaching office.[177]

The Magisterium itself must share some of the blame for this development.[178] As Karl Rahner pointed out some time ago,[179] they have done little to qualify or limit the expectations of the faithful in proposing Church teaching. There is also a deeper issue. This is the reality that we – both leaders and faithful – expect too much certainty from Church teaching and then must tie ourselves in knots trying to explain how the Church can sometimes get it wrong, or risk losing all respect for the notion that authentic teaching is a charism promised by the Spirit to the Church. So, for example, as already indicated, with *Dignatitis Humanae*, strong papal and ecclesial positions about error having no rights, about the desirability of a confessional state and the evils of Church-state separation, were put aside. This was part of what Joseph Ratzinger referred to as the 'counter-syllabus' of the Second Vatican Council, correcting the imbalances found in the Syllabus of Errors of Pius IX (1864) as well as the more general Catholic overreaction to modernism.[180] As Benedict XVI Joseph Ratzinger would go on to explain this kind of significant shift in teaching, as already mentioned, in terms of a 'continuity of principles', with a real discontinuity in terms of concrete historical situations and their requirements.[181] The distinction remains important but its application moot – campaigners for religious freedom in the nineteenth century were in no doubt

177 Congar also observes that: 'we cannot fail to take into account the critical historical study of the magisterium in modern times. Its pretensions seem excessive and unreal' – see Carroll, op. cit., 39.
178 See O'Hanlon, *Irish Catholicism at a Crossroads*, op. cit., 377–80.
179 In 1977 Rahner pointed out that 'statements of the magisterium, although they make no claim to be definitive, are nonetheless presented in such a way as though they are in fact definitive'; and there is a perception that 'Rome normally presents and pushes doctrinal decisions that are *per se* reformable as though there were no doubt whatsoever about their definitive correctness and as though any further discussion about the matter by Catholic theologians would be inappropriate' – 'Open Questions in Dogma Considered by the Institutional Church as Definitively Answered', in *Journal of Ecumenical Studies*, spring, 1978, 212 and 221, cited in D. Carroll, op. cit.
180 Joseph Cardinal Ratzinger, *Principles for Catholic Theology: Building Stones for a Fundamental Theology*, San Francisco, CA: Ignatius, 1987, original German 1982, 381–82. See also International Theological Commission, *Theology Today*, 2012, n. 55; Gerry O'Hanlon, 'Religious Freedom', *The Furrow*, 64, February 2013, 67–77, at 71.
181 Pope Benedict XVI, Address to the Roman Curia, 22 December 2005; O'Hanlon, *Religious Freedom*, op. cit., 76–77.

that they were being opposed on grounds of principle, as Joseph Komonchak points out, and not, as Ratzinger suggests, because of the association of religious freedom with agnosticism or relativism. A different approach is the one adopted by the German bishops in a 1967 letter where they pointed out that it is a fact that there has been error in non-defined magisterial teaching. Hence, it would be intolerable if on all contemporary issues they were expected to speak out with absolute certitude, and if the only alternatives were to speak authoritatively in an absolute way or to keep silence. They argued that this would interfere with their duty to give guidance on topical issues, and so they made clear that on contemporary issues they aim to speak authoritatively but with a certain provisionality.[182]

Over time issues mature and reach definitive status – witness our development in sensibility about the morality of slavery, witness the almost universal acceptance by Catholics of the Creed and defined teaching. This is what is meant by the development of doctrine – which includes of course moral teaching (SF, 72–3). In the meantime we must rest content with a wisdom which is open to correction, and is helped towards maturity by public debate and discussion.[183] Historian and cultural commentator Michael Lacy puts this well – we are part of a culture now which values freedom highly and will not accept truths solely on the say-so of authorities, but which expects persuasive evidence of appropriate consultation and respects individual conscience. This of course is due not least to the chastening experience of Europeans in the twentieth century of the dangers of blind obedience. In this context, Lacy argues, it is better to speak of 'selective Catholicism', rather than the more pejorative 'à la carte Catholicism'.[184]

---

182 Francis A. Sullivan, *Magisterium: Teaching Authority in the Catholic Church*, Dublin: Gill & Macmillan, 1983, 156–57.

183 See in particular the lucid exposition by Patrick Hannon, 'Free Speech in the Church?', *The Furrow*, 63, June 2012, 259–68.

184 Michael J. Lacy, 'The Problem of Authority and its Limits', in Michael J. Lacy and Francis Oakley (eds), *The Crisis of Authority in Catholic Modernity*, Oxford: Oxford University Press, 2011, 1–25, at note 5, p. 22. Lacy notes the way civil authorities are expected to prepare and reference the ground for their rulings which need to be '… accompanied by reasons and assurances that relevant matters have been investigated, appropriate bodies of knowledge have been tapped, interested parties have been canvassed, and the likely consequences of the rule are understood and have been prepared for'(9). This culture of due diligence and accountability affects the way people listen to Church teaching.

It would help, then, if the papal Magisterium showed itself to be more explicitly attentive to these differentiations in its utterances, and showed more evidence of encouragement of and attention to the input of other actors. One thinks, for example, of a more constructively critical input from bishops and their conferences, so that one could speak with more confidence about the trustworthiness of the 'ordinary Magisterium' and the 'universal ordinary Magisterium', knowing that local bishops were making more than a simply deferential contribution. And one thinks above all of the structured input of the faithful, through the likes of regular synods, so that there is a real and transparent valuing of the 'sense of the faithful'.

This is exactly the direction that Pope Francis is now taking with his emphasis on a 'synodal Church', in which decision-making is decentralised, the voice of all is listened too, and a process of discernment rather than a simple 'command and obey' model is used to formulate and then confirm by reception the authenticity of Church teaching. Francis is clear that 'thinking with the Church' means more than obeying the pope and hierarchy: it means also listening carefully to the 'sense of the faithful' and heeding the expertise of theologians.[185] And it would be entirely within the spirit of the feel Francis has for 'the peripheries', to include among the faithful those who have lapsed from practice due to difficulty with current Church teaching and practice. In this context one could honour the call of the distinguished public figure from Northern Ireland, Denis Bradley, when he urges the Catholic Church to consult what he calls the 'unfaithful' if it is to properly renew itself.[186] In using the term 'unfaithful' Bradley clearly intended no disparagement, but rather a recognition of the ongoing value of critical voices which have been alienated, often due to the lack of a forum to discuss contested issues.

There is a loss of credibility when too much is taken on by the centre and the experience of the periphery is not recognised. This over-stretching is counter-productive, leading to the 'anti-Roman

---

185 See Interview and practice of the Synod on the Family.
186 Denis Bradley, *The Irish News*, 4 August 2017.

affect' that von Balthasar decried. The situation is not helped by relying solely on the observation that people don't understand, it must be explained better to them. Might it not also be the case that non-reception should give pause for thought, for re-examination, as it did, according to Newman, in the Arian debates of the fourth century, when the laity were on the correct side of the argument against many of their bishops? In this context the words of Joseph Ratzinger are apt: 'Criticism of Papal pronouncements will be possible and even necessary, to the degree that they lack support in the Scripture and the Creed, that is, in the faith of the whole Church. When neither consensus of the whole Church is had, nor clear evidence from the sources is available, a definitive decision is not possible. Were one formally to take place, while conditions for such were lacking, the question would have to be raised concerning its legitimacy'.[187] I think as well of the Melkite Patriarch Maximos Saïgh's wise saying at the Second Vatican Council, 'Repressed truth turns poisonous'.[188]

The search for truth and meaning is intrinsically human, and the gift of authoritative magisterial teaching is a blessing bestowed on the Church. But it runs the risk of a kind of false absolutisation if it is understood too simplistically. It is not the case that the pope, for example, has a kind of 'direct line' to God that may dispense with the ordinary human and revealed means to attain truth – that close listening to human experience, that clear position of being a servant to God's word. The Church must learn as well as teach, and its teaching comes from learning.[189] Obedience, then, is not mindless, even while dissent should not be reckless or wilful. Catholics have far more in common with each other – and indeed with other Christians – than what divides them, and, again, the old

---

187 Cited by Francis A. Sullivan, op. cit., 209, from Ratzinger's *Das Neue Volk Gottes,* Dusseldorf: Patmos, 1969, 144.
188 Gerry O'Hanlon SJ, *A New Vision for the Catholic Church: A View from Ireland,* Dublin: Columba Press, 2011, 54.
189 Gerard Mannion, 'A Teaching Church That Learns? Discerning "Authentic" Teaching in our Times', in Lacy and Oakley, op. cit., 161–91. Also, from a philosophical perspective and with reference to the Church's need to learn about handling conflict from secular liberal democracies, as well as its need to act as a kind of Socratic midwife in its teaching role, ready to speak in the polyphony of different styles, see Patrick Riordan SJ, 'A Blessed Rage for the Common Good', *Irish Theological Quarterly,* 76, 2011, 3–19.

patristic maxim, loosely translated, is apt: In things that are defined, unity; in things that are still open, freedom; and in everything, love (*In necessariis, unitas; in dubiis, libertas; et in omnibus caritas*).

Conclusion

I have been suggesting that a synodal Church, with its due esteem for hierarchy, theologians and 'sense of the faithful' as sources of truth, is more likely to lead to sound doctrine that is both consistent with the Tradition and responsive to the signs of the times. This will mean moving away from a notion of Tradition that is something exclusively fixed and immutable, a propositional deposit of faith fully revealed from the start. It will mean moving towards, ironically, the more traditional notion of Tradition, that sees it as developing in response to our encounter with the mystery of the person of Jesus Christ in different stages of our own historical growth as individuals and cultures, under the guidance of the Spirit.

Already within Scripture and in the early Church we see this developmental notion of Tradition: If Jesus held firm by the law of Moses, still he did not hesitate from expanding and developing it – now, I say to you, you must love not just your neighbour, but also your enemy; the sins of the fathers and mothers are not borne by the children; salvation is for all, not just the Jews; and, by the fourth century, the orthodox (now traditional) doctrine of the identity of Jesus is expressed by the term 'consubstantial' – a non-scriptural neologism, an apparent disruption with the past, which the gifted, pious, but ultimately heterodox Arius rejects, because he sees it as untrue to scriptural and traditional teaching.

Newman scholar Dermot Roantree, in a series of blogs in 2017, points helpfully to an underlying dynamic here.[190] He draws on the distinction in Bernard Lonergan between two different mentalities or states of consciousness – classicism and historical consciousness. The former stresses what is permanent, immutable, the fixed identity

---

190 Dermot Roantree, the greatest of these is charity, not clarity – http://www.jesuit.ie/blog/dermot-roantree/greatest-charity-not-clarity/; The death penalty and doctrine, Part 1 – http://www.jesuit.ie/blog/dermot-roantree/death-penalty-and-doctrine-part-1/; The death penalty and doctrine, Part 2 – http://www.jesuit.ie/blog/dermot-roantree/death-penalty-doctrine-part- 2/

of human nature, so that tradition is that fixed body of doctrine which is normative now and always, without that creative and active receptivity which is involved in the act of handing on of Tradition. In this context the only historical change in Tradition that is possible is that of allowing the light of understanding to fall gradually on what was obscurely believed in the past. Historical consciousness, on the other hand, sees human nature and identity as constitutively historical, so that there is always need of a hermeneutic, a philosophy of interpretation, to navigate between the Scylla of a fundamentalist objectivity and the Charybdis of a rootless relativism. In this context doctrinal change may be not just developmental in a seemingly straightforward organically, evolutionary way, but may also be corrective, so that continuity needs to be sought at deeper levels. Roantree notes the temptations of both sides to demonise the other and pleads for the 'principle of charity' that has been frequently invoked in discourse theory: 'The greatest of these is charity, not clarity' is the title of one of his blogs.

It would be good if the Catholic Church could begin to acknowledge more explicitly the reality of doctrinal development. It may be helped to do so by a return to the kind of culture of 'discernment' which is so prominent in the thinking of Pope Francis. In this Francis makes it clear that he is interested not so much in the disjointed transmission of a multitude of doctrines to be insistently imposed (EG, 35) but rather in our encounter with our loving God of mercy in Jesus Christ. This involves the non-exact science of relationship and it is precisely in this arena that expertise is shared between the most illiterate and most educated of believers – we are all called into relationship with God, and in what matters most we all try to make existential decisions, not from a pre-written script but according to a conscience that is informed by, among other sources, Church teaching. It will help to examine the notion of discernment a little more closely.

CHAPTER SIX

The Art of Communal Discernment

It seemed good to us and the Holy Spirit. (Acts 15:28)

Why talk about Discernment?[191]

In his concluding address to Part One of the Synod of Bishops on the Family, Pope Francis remarked that we now have 'one year to mature, with true spiritual discernment, the proposed ideas and to find concrete solutions to so many difficulties and innumerable challenges that families must confront' (Concluding Discourse, 18 October 2014). The synod reconvened for Part Two in October 2015 with a view to finding these concrete solutions, with the thorny issues of the admission of the divorced and remarried to sacramental communion and the attitude to gay faithful to the forefront. In the event, as we know, it proved too difficult to move any more decisively on the issue of homosexuality, but decisions were taken around the issue of the divorced and remarried.[192]

The Pope, as is clear from the totality of his concluding address (and not just this one quotation), understood this synodal, collegial process, and the consultation of all the faithful which informed it, as being one of discernment.

This is not so surprising coming from a Jesuit pope steeped in the tradition of St Ignatius. In his first substantive interview (Interview), given over three meetings during August 2013, to Antonio Spadara SJ, editor of *La Civiltà Cattolica*, and published in September 2013), when asked what element of Ignatian spirituality helped him

---

191 See Gerry O'Hanlon, 'Discernment and the Synod on the Family', *Doctrine and Life*, 65, September 2015, 9–20; The Limerick Synod, *The Furrow*, 66, June 2015, 320–29, at 325–29.
192 O'Hanlon, 'The Joy of Love – *Amoris Laetitia*', *The Furrow*, 67, June 2016, 328–36.

to live out his ministry, he replied: 'discernment', and went on to express his belief that while 'many think that changes and reforms can take place in a short time, I believe that that we always need to lay foundations for real, effective change. And this is the time of discernment'. Similarly he uses the term discernment, and its cognate forms, over twenty times in *Evangelii Gaudium*.

Discernment for the Pope involves attention to the signs of the times, while remaining faithful to the counter-cultural message of the gospels – so much is clear already from his closing address at the synod. And we may also conclude that it involves elements such as the exercise of episcopal and papal authority, theological input, fidelity to the Scriptures and Tradition, and obedience to Church teaching. Of course, Church teaching for Francis allows for real input in formation and reception of teaching to the *sensus fidei* of the faithful and the processes of communication and assessment of public opinion which this involves – a clear departure in practice from recent ecclesial ways of proceeding, even if faithful to a long tradition.

However, the Pope seems to imply that somehow discernment itself is the key factor in integrating all these elements and for this reason I think it worthwhile to examine in a little more detail what he might mean by discernment.

What is Discernment?
Discernment is, emphatically, not something invented by St Ignatius of Loyola. Rather it is already present throughout the Hebrew Testament (see, for example, the need to differentiate between true and false prophets), the New Testament (see especially the Letters of Paul – '… the discernment of spirits' in 1 Corinthians 12:10, and the account in Acts 15 of the Council of Jerusalem). It is also present in the rhapsodic approach to God in patristic literature and, in particular, the spiritual introspection of Augustine's Confessions; the decision-making of monastic chapters and of religious founders like St Dominic and St Francis of Assisi; and the many councils of the Church, both local and ecumenical.[193] The original contribution

193 See Hinze, 2016, op. cit., 135–37, for a brief survey of the topic of discernment in
    Christianity.

of Ignatius, drawing primarily on his own experience, was to draw together the different elements of discernment and present them in a systematic way for practical use. He did this primarily in an individual context, as his Spiritual Exercises make clear. However, as the practice of Ignatius and his founding nine companions, recorded in the *Deliberatio primorum Patrum* (The Deliberation of the First Fathers), also makes clear, discernment may also be used communally and, in modern times, has increasingly been so used.

At the heart of discernment is the search for the will of God, for 'God's point of view', as Pope Francis puts it (Interview). It is true that God's will is known in a general way to all believers through the teaching of Scripture and the Church. Nonetheless, life in all its singularities, ambiguities and choices between good and evil but also, and more pertinently for the Christian disciple, between good and better, throws up serious questions of truth and value which must be decided upon afresh and for which there is no obvious blueprint to provide answers. I am not speaking here about the more obvious, common-sense tasks of life (for example, fixing a puncture) or, indeed, issues susceptible to technical solution, where it is inappropriate to use the language of discernment.[194] These questions arise with existential sharpness at particular times in life – should I get married or enter religious life, should the Church admit the divorced and remarried to sacramental communion or continue with the status quo?

At such serious, existential moments Ignatius trusts that God does not simply leave us to our own devices but, through the process of prayerful discernment, invites us to ask for the help of the Holy Spirit, who 'guides you into all the truth' (Jn 16:13), in order to discover God's hopes and dreams for us in this concrete situation. What is at issue here is what Ladislas Orsy, in a communal context, refers to 'as the working of God's grace in a community'.[195] Ignatius

194 This may explain the relative absence of the term discernment in *Laudato Si'* (2015), the papal encyclical on Care for Our Common Home, where many of the issues are primarily technical and the reality – if not the terminology – of discernment only come into prominence when Francis speaks of the required ecological conversion. It does seem that Ignatius himself, as he went on in life, increasingly found it easier to find God in small as well as big matters, but this extended use of discernment is not our primary concern here.

195 Ladislas Orsy SJ, *Probing the Spirit, A Theological Evaluation of Communal Discernment*, New Jersey: Dimension Books, 1976, 13.

himself, in the individual context of the Spiritual Exercises, notes that the Creator 'deals directly with the creature, and the creature directly with his Creator and Lord' (Sp. Ex., 15).

Ignatius goes on to specify three particular 'times' or 'modes' of decision-making in this graced context.[196] The first – and rarest – time is 'when God our Lord so moves and draws the will that, without doubting or the power of doubting, the faithful person follows what is shown, as St Paul and St Matthew did in following Christ our Lord' (Sp. Ex., 175). Some – including Karl Rahner – equate this 'time' to what Ignatius refers to as 'consolation without cause', but Toner rejects this exclusive equation.[197]

The second, much more common, time of decision-making is 'when sufficient light and understanding are gathered, through experiences of consolations and desolations and through experience of discerning diverse spirits' (Sp. Ex., 176). What Ignatius is referring to here is not simply at the level of ordinary emotion, feeling, imagination and desire, but rather, inclusive of these, at a level where the spirit is engaged, where explicitly faith and spiritual reality are being considered. In that context consolation will refer to the kind of gifts of Spirit outlined in Galatians 5:22–23: 'love, joy, peace, patience, kindness, goodness, faithfulness, gentleness, self-control'. Ignatius himself writes in terms of the soul being inflamed with love, or when one sheds tears, or: '... I call consolation every increase of faith, hope, and love, and all interior joy that invites and attracts to what is heavenly and to the salvation of one's soul by filling it with and quiet in its Creator and Lord' (Sp. Ex., 316).

For the person or community on the path towards God, then, consolation gives a sense of encouragement and hope. Desolation, on the other hand, causes discouragement and despair. It involves 'darkness of the soul, turmoil of spirit, inclination to what is low and earthly, restlessness rising from many disturbances and temptations which lead us to want of faith, want of hope, want of love. The soul is wholly slothful, tepid, sad, and separated, as it were, from its Creator and Lord' (Sp. Ex., 317). Part of the genius of Ignatius

---

196 Jules J. Toner SJ, *Discerning God's Will*, St Louis, MO: Institute of Jesuit Sources, 1991, 102–273.
197 Ibid., 114–18.

was precisely to propose the kind of subtle 'language of the heart' which was able to help others to interpret these 'movements of the spirit' and also to distinguish between a false kind of consolation (a sense of peace to the complacent, who were in fact hiding from a deeper call) and the possible positive effects of desolation (the call of conscience, for example, in someone going from bad to worse).[198] Pope Francis, in the same closing address to the first session of the synod, gave a masterly exposition of this interplay of consolation and desolation as it occurred in the synodal interactions, noting in particular desolations and temptations characteristic of both the 'right' and the 'left'.

The third time of decision-making is when a person or community is not stirred up by consolation and desolation but 'has free and tranquil use of his natural powers' (Sp. Ex., 177). This is a time of reasoning, of searching for insight, of weighing up pros and cons, always under the influence of the Holy Spirit.

While the authoritative Ignatian commentator Jules Toner argues for, in principle, the distinction and autonomy of the three times or modes of 'election', nonetheless he is at one with most other commentators in agreeing that in practice 'a combination of the second and third modes is desirable for greater security' and 'even requisite'.[199] The term 'felt knowledge' is, accordingly, an apt description of what discernment is about.[200]

Once a decision has been made, Ignatius notes the need to ask for the grace of 'confirmation' – again, while one may distinguish the intellectual and volitional components of this confirmation,[201] it is often the case that both are present as the combination of compelling evidence and a sense of peace yield to a feeling of completeness. Ignatius believes that what is being sought in discernment is a gift from God, and so he presupposes that the individual or community in question will have the right dispositions to facilitate the reception

---

198 See Chapter Four above for some more on the possible positive function of desolation, and the suggestions of Hinze in this respect, going beyond the stated position of Ignatius – Hinze, 2016, op. cit., 85–7.
199 Toner, op. cit., 254.
200 See Eugene Duffy, 'Assembly or Synod?', *The Furrow*, 63, June 2012, 295–303, at 301; and see note 17 for a helpful bibliography.
201 Toner, op. cit., chapter 12.

of this gift. By this he is referring for the need to pray, to ask in particular for freedom from all bias and self-delusion, not to mention social and cultural pressures. This Ignatian anthropology is grounded – as well as an appreciation of our natural gifts of intellect and reason, and their openness to God's calling, there is also a recognition of the bias of our natural and sinful self-interest. This includes our resistances to the concerns and voices of others, our propensities to rationalisation and self-deception, to rigidities and compulsions. The more open ('indifferent') we are, to others and God, the more likely we are to make good decisions. A skilled guide or facilitator will know how to lead an individual or group, through prayer, well-judged 'time-outs' and a process of reflection on reasons and feelings to a point where God's word becomes clearer.

What Issues Arise?
Several issues arise from this account of Ignatian communal discernment, in particular as it applies to what is going on in the Church in these times.

1. THEOLOGICAL QUESTIONS AND, IN PARTICULAR, THE SENSE OF THE FAITH
Underlying Ignatian discernment is the confidence that God is involved in our world, with individuals and groups, that God labours in all creation (Sp. Ex., 236), and that divine Providence through God's positive and permissive will, with our cooperation and in spite of our resistance, is bringing about the Kingdom. This confidence requires theological underpinning: Aquinas provided this by wrestling with the interplay between primary and secondary causality, Lonergan took this up with his attention to transcendent and contingent causality, and we now need more theological work to be done for our own day on this topic.

The challenge is to do justice to the relationship between grace and freedom: as the pope says, 'our life is not given to us like an opera libretto, in which all is written down' (Interview), a blueprint notion of the will of God; but nor can we simply take up a Deist position which suggests that while God created the world now it is left to us (as 'adults') to get on with things on our own. Somehow we need to do justice to both sides of this relationship: Orsy suggests[202] the analogy of 'trusted friend' as more fitting than that of parent/child, or indeed teacher/pupil. Von Balthasar has spoken about a play that is co-written (and co-acted) by God and us. In any case any such analogy has to be inserted into a narrative that takes more precise account of the findings of evolutionary cosmology and biology, as well of the human sciences like psychology and sociology. At stake is our image of God and, to use the traditional language, the relationship between the natural and supernatural.

Of more immediate need is a theological grasp of the relationship between discernment and the 'sense of the faith' spoken about in the Second Vatican Council (see especially LG, 12). *Sensus Fidei in the Life of the Church* is most helpful in this respect.[203] The authors speak of the *sensus fidei* – of the individual and then of the community, the *sensus fidelium* – in terms of a certain instinct or intuition given to individuals at baptism, developing into a mature capacity and sensibility through their adult lives, and issuing in an ability to then discern God's will. This instinct, as I mentioned, is distinguished from objective knowledge: instead it is spoken of in terms of a certain 'co-naturality' of the type that obtains, for example, between friends – in other words, as in *Dei Verbum*, the approach is to go deeper than propositional knowledge and to move into the realm of mystery proper to the personal, including the realms of desire and feeling. Nonetheless, the sense of faith does have a major role in the development of Christian belief, doctrine, moral teaching and practice (DV, 72–3).

As already indicated, the document notes that this sense of the faith cannot simply be equated to majority public opinion (many times in the history of salvation it was the prophet or the minority who held on to truth) and that it remains the duty of the Magisterium to discern the authenticity of the sense of the faith. Nonetheless the public exchange of opinion will be one of the best sources of gauging the authentic *sensus fidelium,* as will the likes of councils

202 Orsy, 1976, op. cit., 75.
203 See International Theological Commission, *'Sensus Fidei' in the Life of the Church*, 2014 – authorised for publication by Cardinal Mueller, Prefect of the Congregation of the Doctrine of the Faith.

and synods, in particular when the right dispositions are present in participants. And, in tune with Pope Francis, the authors note the particular importance to be given to the periphery, to the voice of the poor, to popular devotion.

This analysis chimes well with what has already been said about discernment. Reasoning is important, but so too is 'knowledge of the heart' and the sense that, in faith, we are being led into a deeper grasp of the truth, so that 'the *sensus fidei* needs to be viewed within the context of history, a history in which the Holy Spirit makes each day a day to hear the voice of the Lord afresh (Heb 3:7–15; SF, 68). In this context the skills of discernment will enable the individual, the community and the Magisterium to make wise choices on the basis of this gift of the sense of faith. The underlying epistemology recalls the grappling of Aquinas with the relationship between intellect and will, Lonergan in his marrying of the realms of theory and interiority, Rahner with his focus on mystagogy and 'consolation without cause', and von Balthasar with his insistence on prayer and poetry as theological sources and resources.

2. 'NOISY DISCERNMENT'

It might be objected that while the nuanced process of discernment as outlined above might have some traction in a relatively homogeneous, tight-knit community (such as a community of vowed religious), where one can presuppose a certain amount of common skills and requisite dispositions, it is entirely different when one attempts to apply it to the Church at large. Can discernment really function in the hurly-burly of public debate, strongly held contrasting opinions, real conflict and relative ignorance of the subtleties of discernment-theory which characterise the context of the Synod on the Family?

Toner is interesting in this context. He notes the basic Ignatian pre-condition that we do 'our very best' to be open to the Holy Spirit and to proceed intelligently, and says that in those circumstances there is no reason to confine spiritual discernment of God's will 'to a psychological and spiritual elite … this means that you and I and the next person can have just as much confidence of finding God's will as Ignatius of Loyola, Teresa of Avila, Dominic, Catherine of

Siena, and others …'.[204] It will, on the other hand, be helpful to look for skilled guidance if this is available – so, in the context of the synod, not just group facilitation skills but also skills in communal discernment itself.

This basic position harmonises well with two observations of *Sensus Fidei* – the authors reference the Angelus remarks by Pope Francis when he quoted the words of a humble, elderly woman he once met: 'If the Lord did not forgive everything, the world would not exist', noting that this enables a real discernment arising out of the *sensus fidei* (SF, 2); and, later on, they refer to the famous example quoted by Newman where the faith of the laity was to the forefront defending the orthodox position on the divinity of Christ in the periods between the ecumenical councils of Nicea and Constantinople in the fourth century (SF, 26).

Pope Francis himself, as his conduct at the last synod clearly indicates, is comfortable with this kind of 'noisy discernment'.[205]

3. DEBATE AS WELL AS DIALOGUE

Many commentators[206] note that dialogue (a careful listening to the position of the other) rather than debate (which would engage in argumentation) is the preferred way of proceeding in discernment. Again, I think that this can be understood in an overly purist way which would, in effect, rule out the kind of arguing, gossiping, alliances, conflicts, compromises and political intrigues which characterise all human attempts at collaboration on important matters and which have been abundantly present in ecclesial synods and ecumenical councils of the past. Richard Gaillardetz expresses this well:

At an ecumenical council, saints and sinners, the learned and the ignorant, gather together. They share their faith, voice their concerns, argue, gossip, forge alliances and compromises, enter into political intrigue, rise above the intrigue to discern the movements of the Spirit, worry about the great tradition in which their identity is rooted, seek to

204 Toner, op. cit., 312.
205 A phrase coined by a colleague, Brian Grogan SJ, to whom many thanks.
206 See, in particular, Jules J. Toner, 'A Method for Communal Discernment of God's Will', *Studies in the Spirituality of Jesuits*, Vol. iii, n 4, September 1971, especially 137–38.

understand the demands of the present moments and hope for a better future.[207]

What is important, surely, is an attempt by the participants themselves in any communal discernment to seek the Holy Spirit in all this, which will certainly involve an attempt to listen as openly as possible to the views of others and, above all, to be open to what Francis has called the God of surprises. This is surely what happened at the Second Vatican Council – the council fathers were by no means expecting much out of the ordinary when they gathered in Rome for the start of the council, and yet, over the months and years, they had an experience which allowed them to echo the words of the Council of Jerusalem: 'It seemed good to us and the Holy Spirit' (Acts 15:28).

4. LIMITS OF DISCERNMENT

Unity and peace are gifts of the Holy Spirit and so, quite rightly, there is typically a desire among participants in communal discernment to achieve unity and even, if possible, consensus. However, the thrust towards consensus can lead towards the temptation to adopt a kind of lowest common denominator approach. It may be that a consensus is unobtainable at any particular time, but discernment also accommodates the ordinary structures of institutions like synods and councils with their requirements for voting and weighted majorities.

There is a real sense in which truth is not negotiable – it must correspond with reality, and decisions taken to achieve unity and peace at the expense of truth will soon need to be re-examined in order to express what is objectively so. In this sense communal decisions, even those of synods, are authoritative but are not infallible – they are reformable. As human beings we need to respect our creaturely status, which means that we are always searching rather than in full possession of truth, always subject to what Lonergan refers to as the self-corrective process of learning.

Orsy, in this context, notes the 'paradox of peaceful mistakes'[208] by which our infinitely patient and provident God accepts when

207 *America*, 13 February 2012.
208 Orsy, op. cit., 64–68.

we have done our best, even though, at this attempt, we may have failed adequately to address the 'objective world outside of us with its own ruthless demands for truth and purposefulness'.[209] With regard to the Synod on the Family it was desirable that the 'concrete solutions' which Pope Francis had spoken about were found, and within the projected time frame. This gave the Church confidence that this 'new' way of proceeding synodically and by discernment was working.

However it is also important to recognise that while deadlines and concrete outputs are helpful, they are not normally absolutes: we may not force the hand of God or do violence to the consciences of individuals and of the group in insisting that the Holy Spirit act according to our own expectations. It may be that we need more theological research on certain issues, a wider and deeper consultation of the faithful, before decisions can be reached with peace, if not unanimity. However, we should never simply procrastinate in order to avoid hard decisions – this would result in a false unity and an erosion of confidence in the process.

5. AUTHORITY AND DISCERNMENT

Sensus Fidei is clear that it is the function of the Magisterium to discern the authentic 'sense of the faith' and, implicitly, to teach authoritatively. There are two contrasting challenges arising from this position, particularly in a culture where authority in both secular and ecclesial circles is viewed with suspicion and even antipathy.

The first comes to those of us who are liberals and who by instinct value the free expression of opinion and the attainment of truth and not just consensus. Can we see the need for authority not simply as a coercive external force but as essential internally to any community, a means by which a common vision may be preserved and flourish, with the power (including legal powers) to ground its authority? And can we accept that, in the short term (and we always live time that is eschatological, which means not in the fullness of time), less than perfect decisions need to be taken to hold our group together, without ever giving up on the unceasing

209 Ibid., 65.

quest for fuller truth and always valuing the voices of dissent? The second challenge is to those of us more inclined to be at ease with the status quo. Why need we remain with a notion of Magisterium and ecclesial governance that is exclusively male and exclusively restricted to the ordained? Pope Francis himself has spoken of the need to have women in decision-making positions, while there have been serious questions raised about the legitimacy of the restrictive Canon 129 of the New Code in terms of lay participation in decision-making.[210] Why cannot we begin to move towards not just a consultative but also a deliberative role for laity in the Church, consonant with their share, through Baptism, the priestly, prophetic and *kingly* (my emphasis) office of Jesus Christ? The Synod on the Family has drawn particular attention to this need for a more central role for lay men and women in tackling issues which so centrally affect them.

Conclusion
The synodal, collegial reshaping of the Catholic Church is a radical and momentous sign of our times. A greater appreciation of the art (not science)[211] of discernment will help enormously towards a successful outcome, provided we does not treat it as a kind of panacea and are respectful of its limits. Of course the task is daunting, and, in particular, the fault lines of conflict, division and resistance run deep. However, we can recall that back at the time of our origins as Christians, the Council of Jerusalem, in a collegial, discerning way, tackled with confidence a major issue which threatened to tear the Church apart. Christians are above all people of hope, and '… hope does not disappoint us, because God's love has been poured into our hearts through the Holy Spirit who has been given to us' (Rm 5:5). And, in our own time and country, we can all learn much from the 2016 Synod of Limerick (see Chapter Nine).

210 See Ladislas Orsy, *Receiving the Council,* Collegeville, MN: Liturgical Press, 2009, in particular chapter 3, 'Discourse about the Laity: A Sacred Power', 35–45.
211 See Gerry O'Hanlon, 'The Limerick Synod', *The Furrow,* 66, June 2015, 320–29, and 'Reflections on the Synod', *The Furrow,* 65, December 2014, 583–91.

CHAPTER SEVEN

Governance in
a Synodal Church

*The centralised control from which we suffer, and which
has contributed so greatly to the present crisis of authority,
was built up in less than 100 years. It could be put
into reverse in less than ten.*
(Nicholas Lash, *Theology for Pilgrims*, 2008)

In speaking of an 'entirely synodal church' it is clear that Pope
Francis wants all the faithful to have a say in Church governance, in
what touches their lives. This is based on the teaching of the Second
Vatican Council, with deep roots in Scripture and the Tradition, on
the share of all the baptised in the priestly, prophetic (teaching) and
kingly (governance) roles of Jesus Christ (LG, 10–13). There are
legitimate hopes and fears around this project of a more inclusive
Church at the level of governance.

Some fear that it will lead to polarisation and fragmentation, as has
sometimes been the case in other Christian communities. A strong
central leadership, with expectations of command and control, and
an obedient clergy and laity, had the merit of maintaining unity, even
at the expense of what many experienced as a stifling uniformity. I
have outlined how the culture is no longer sympathetic to such a
model of authority, and, ironically, even those most enthusiastic for
it in the past find themselves suddenly confounded when confronted
with a pope whose decisions they do not like.

We have seen how the Second Vatican Council proposed a more
inclusive model of ecclesial authority – in line with scriptural and

traditional witness – but how quickly, for various reasons, there was a return to the more recent, centralised tradition.[212] The hope is that in his proposals around a synodal Church, with a more inclusive participation in both teaching and governance in a context of open debate, meaningful consultation and discernment, Francis may have retrieved a way forward which is both faithful to our self-understanding as Church and resonant with the signs of our times. How might we envisage governance in a synodal Church in a way that, faithful to the Trinitarian model which is the source of the Church, encourages unity in diversity? What sort of questions and issues emerge?

Overview [213]

Theologically the Second Vatican Council spoke of the Church as a communion, a union of baptised persons in the image of the unity and diversity at the heart of our triune God of Father, Son and Holy Spirit. The People of God are central to this vision, and priests, bishops and pope are leaders in service of the people. Each of the lay faithful shares in the priestly, prophetic and kingly role of Jesus Christ, both within the Church itself and with respect to the secular world. Within this vision collegiality, or, to use the preferred term of Francis, synodality, needs to find expression at all levels, while local Churches are the Body of Christ in their own place and not simply subdivisions of the one, universal Church.

In this context ecclesiologist Richard Gaillardetz[214] can state: 'The pope is neither head of the whole Church, nor bishop of the whole Church. It is Christ and not the bishop of Rome who is head of the Church (cf Ep 1:22 - 3 Col 1:18) ... neither is the pope the bishop of the universal church ... the pope is pope only because he is first the bishop of the local church of Rome, a church which from ancient

212 See Chapter Two above and Gerry O'Hanlon, 'The future of the Catholic Church – a view from Ireland', *Studies,* 99, autumn 2010, 289–301.

213 See Gerry O'Hanlon, 'Whispers of the Spirit – the Church of the Future', *The Furrow,* 64, June 2013, 332–41, at 334–37; 'Irish Catholicism at a Crossroads', *Studies,* 101, winter 2012, 375–86, at 380–83; 'Vatican II as a Resource for the Renewal of the Church in Ireland in the Twenty-First Century', in Dermot A. Lane (ed.), *Vatican II in Ireland, Fifty Years On,* op. cit., 219–36, at 232–35; 'Free Speech in the Church', *Studies,* 105, summer 2016, 199–211.

214 Richard R. Gaillardetz, *By What Authority?,* Collegeville, MN: Liturgical Press, 2003, chapter 4, 63–73.

times was granted a distinctive primacy among the churches'.[215]

The pope, then, is better described not as head of the Church but as pastor of the universal Church in virtue of his role as bishop of the local church of Rome. Gaillardetz goes on to argue that: 'Vatican I taught that it was in his capacity as bishop of Rome that the pope possesses a unique responsibility to preserve and nurture the unity of the faith and the communion of churches', so that 'many theologians now believe that all significant papal actions exercised for the good of the whole church, are, by definition, collegial', and that even when the pope acts 'alone', he does so 'as head of the college of bishops'.[216] It is only in extraordinary circumstances that the pope may intervene in the affairs of a local Church for the sake of the unity of faith and communion of all the Churches.

This theological understanding, as already noted, is very much in harmony with the views of Pope John Paul II in his 1995 encyclical *Ut Unum Sint,* with its preferred use of the title 'bishop of Rome' and its presentation of the papacy as a ministry of service within an ecclesiology of communion and its appeal for help in re-envisaging the role along these lines. It is a theological vision that requires the flesh and bones of appropriate structural, institutional, legal and cultural embodiment at all levels of ecclesial life. And so, we need to give effective and not just affective collegiality to episcopal conferences, to find ways to bring about a more collegial form of universal government in the Church, and restore decision-making powers to laity (which will require a change to Canon 129).[217]

This more participative form of universal government requires more collegial structures in Rome itself, the more frequent use of synods at all levels, and may even, in the medium term, require the convocation of an ecumenical council to address the major issues that face the Church, not least to resolve the residual ambiguity surrounding the primatial and collegial aspects of papacy.

In this context it is worth quoting at some length the remarks

215 Ibid., 69.
216 Ibid., 70.
217 See Gerry O'Hanlon, *A New Vision for the Catholic Church: A View from Ireland,* Dublin: Columba Press, 2011; and 'Razing the Ramparts – A Theological Reflection on Papal Primacy', *Doctrine and Life,* 62, July-August 2012, 35–52.

originally made by distinguished theologian Nicholas Lash in 2003, drawing on the inspiration of the Second Vatican Council and, in particular, on the contributions of the Melkite Patriarch Maximos IV Saïgh, as well as on the subsequent reflections by the likes of Archbishop John Quinn of San Francisco:

> What we need, and what (in my judgement) it is not unrealistic to hope for, is the election of a pope who, broadly sharing Archbishop Quinn's diagnosis of the problem, establishes a commission, which the pope would chair, whose members would be perhaps 40 or 50 diocesan bishops, drawn from every corner of the world, and which would be advised by officials of the Roman Curia, and by historians, theologians and canon lawyers from outside Rome (many of whom, of course, might be laypeople, women as well as men). The task of this commission would be to draw up proposals for the transfer of governance in the church from pope and Curia to pope and bishops, through the establishment of a standing synod whose members would be diocesan bishops and whose work would be assisted by the offices of a Curia so reformed as to function, not as an instrument of governance, but as a service of administration. The work of this commission, when completed, would then be submitted to the worldwide episcopate for comment, and, presumably revision, before receiving from the pope its final ratification. The centralised control from which we suffer, and which has contributed so greatly to the present crisis of authority, was built up in less than 100 years. It could be put into reverse in less than ten.[218]

Lash's proposals, or some variant of same, have great merit. One could, perhaps, widen the circle of advisers envisaged to include political scientists and experts in governance and organisational theory. One might, as well, wonder whether the 'standing synod' might not include lay people, men and women, who might or might not be appointed as cardinals.

It is worth noting in this context the observations of canon lawyer

218 N. Lash, *Theology for Pilgrims*, London: Darton, Longman & Todd, 2008, 239.

and former Irish president Mary McAleese. She observes that in the period up to the reforms of Francis, with that unresolved mixture of monarchy and collegiality characteristic of the First and Second Vatican Councils respectively, what we have in the Catholic Church theologically and canonically '... is in effect, arguably, constitutionally incoherent'.[219] And she notes that there is a wealth of suggestions from canonists, theologians and others about possible models of government which would be more collegial, in a context where '... today's increasingly secular structures make solitary centralised authorities look like an ebb tide'. She proposes the designation of '... the Synod of Bishops as a standing decision-making body representative of the College of Bishops (whether by partial or full delegation). The Synod's powers would be delegated by the Synod Bishops and not those delegated by the Pope.'[220]

Implicit in all this is reform of the Roman Curia. Jesuit political scientist Thomas Reese does well here to distinguish between two types of reform: better management and comprehensive reform. Under the rubric of management Reese refers to issues like financial corruption, sexual impropriety, petty infighting and the leaking of documents. Under the rubric of comprehensive reform there arises the basic need to see the function of the Curia in service of the pope as head of the college of bishops – 'it should be organised as a civil service and not part of the hierarchy of the Church'.[221]

The notion of learning from others, in particular from 'the world', is taken up by Reese in another reflection. He notes how much the present Vatican structure is based on the secular political field of Roman and later imperial and monarchical times, and says that 'to make the church more collegial, the Vatican should once again adopt practices of the secular political world'.[222] The tired old objection that 'the Church is not a democracy' fails to take account of Reese's

219 Mary McAleese, 'Open the lines of contact', *The Tablet*, 20 October 2012, 14–15. For a fuller account, see her *Quo Vadis? Collegiality in the Code of Canon Law*, Dublin: Columba Press, 2012, especially 11–19; 153–61.
220 Mary McAleese, 'The centre cannot hold', *The Tablet*, 8 March 2014, 11–13.
221 Thomas J. Reese, 'How Pope Francis can reform the Vatican Curia', *National Catholic Reporter*, 25 March 2013; see also Robert Mickens, 'A house that needs putting in order', *The Tablet*, 16 March 2013, 6–7.
222 Thomas J. Reese, 'Reforming the Vatican, What the Church Can Learn from Other Institutions', *Commonweal*, 25 April 2008, 15–17.

argument that the Church has always learned from secular reality, not to mention that there are many democratic elements present in the Church from the very start (the presence of the Holy Spirit in all believers, the notion of leadership as service, the taking of decisions in collegial fashion), as time progressed (the election of bishops in the first millennium) and in the very teachings of the Second Vatican Council (the Church as the People of God, with all the baptised sharing in the priestly, prophetic and royal or governing roles of Christ, the centrality of the 'sense of the faithful'). Reese notes that 'the contemporary papacy rules the Church with powers that would be the envy of any absolute monarch: the pope holds supreme legislative, executive, and judicial authority with few checks on his power'.[223] Reese suggests various concrete reforms to give substance to the notion of more collegial governance, one of them being an independent judiciary (perhaps made up of retired bishops) which would obviate the abuse that allows the executive to indict, prosecute, judge and sentence a defendant – a way of operating that in secular reality would be considered a violation of basic rights and of due process. Reese goes on to maintain, as have many others, that '... the treatment of theologians accused of dissent by the Congregation of the Doctrine of the Faith (CDF) is one of the scandals of the Church'. One of the important issues at this level is an updating of the procedures of the CDF to bring them in line with the best practice of natural justice in the secular sphere.[224]

I have already noted the rather fearful and defensive attitude that took hold of the Church in the middle period after the Second Vatican Council. There was the anxiety about Liberation Theology in the 1980s, the silencing or cautioning of dozens of theologians, including Sean Fagan in Ireland, and other authors (including again several religious in Ireland, the best known perhaps being the case of Redemptorist priest Tony Flannery).[225] Then there was the

223 Reese, 'Reforming the Vatican, What the Church Can Learn from Other Institutions', op. cit., p. 15.

224 Orsy, 2009, op. cit., chapter 7; also Bradford E. Hinze, 'A Decade of Disciplining Theologians', in Richard R. Gaillardetz (ed.), When the Magisterium Intervenes, Collegeville, MN: Liturgical Press, 2012, 3–39, and Jim Corkery SJ, 'Speak Freely – but watch your back! Dissent and Dissenters in the Catholic Church Today', Doctrine and Life, 62, December 2012, 10–22.

225 See Hinze, 'A Decade of Disciplining Theologians', in Gaillardetz (ed.), op. cit., 3–39; Gabriel Daly, The Church – Always in Need of Reform, Dublin: Dominican Publications, 2015,

attempt to remove certain issues from discussion of any kind and the introduction of the term 'definitively taught' to cover something like the ordination of women (see Chapter Eight). Side by side with all this was a growing unease with the methods and procedures of the CDF, with its excessive powers.[226] In a forensic analysis canonist Ladislas Orsy judged that their revised 1997 norms did not meet the requirement of justice for our day.[227] Irish Carmelite theologian Christopher O'Donnell noted that 'the rather obsessive secrecy surrounding much Church consultation is not helpful'.[228] This was an era when it really did seem as if there was little respect for 'Her Majesty's Opposition', to use Rahner's phrase.

The reopening of windows by Pope Francis has been experienced by many, then, as a great relief. He has declared, for example, that he wants Roman congregations to be institutions of help to the bishops and pope, not institutions of censorship, noting that many cases of supposed lack of orthodoxy should be handled locally by conferences of bishops and not by Rome.[229] In this context one could envisage that the CDF might revert to the role, originally intended for it by Paul VI when he established it (replacing the draconian Holy Office), of encouraging responsible theological debate within the Church. And there is the invitation for all the baptised, in accordance with their gifts, to engage in that responsible conversation about faith and the Church about which Rahner spoke back in the 1950s, a conversation entirely compatible with both criticism and loyalty, and of huge benefit to the Church in its mission to grow in truth, love and holiness and be a more effective sign to the world of God's Kingdom. It is in this context that Francis, in his fiftieth anniversary address, could dare to speak of the hope that the Church might become a banner, an inspiration to a world that values participation,

chapters 7 and 9; Tony Flannery, *A Question of Conscience*, Dublin: Londubh Books, 2013.

226 Thomas Reese noted in 2008 that '... the contemporary papacy rules the church with powers that would be the envy of any absolute monarch: the pope holds supreme legislative, executive, and judicial authority with few checks of power' and goes on to state that '... the treatment of theologians accused of dissent by the Congregation for the Doctrine of the Faith (CDF) is one of the scandals of the church' – *Commonweal*, 25 April 2008, 15–17.

227 See Ladislas Orsy, *Receiving the Council*, Collegeville, MN: Liturgical Press, 2009, chapter 7, especially 102–4.

228 Christopher O'Donnell, O Carm, *Ecclesia, A Theological Encyclopedia*, Collegeville, MN: Liturgical Press, 1996, 136 (article on Dissent).

229 Pope Francis, 'A Big Heart Open to God', Jesuit Interview, 2013.

solidarity and transparency but does not always achieve them.[230]
Implicit too is a change of culture, from what Jesuit clinical psychologist Brendan Callaghan has referred to as a dominant, dysfunctional clericalism, deeply authoritarian and defensive, which encouraged secrecy and relied on the collusion and co-responsibility of all of us. Callaghan describes the 'gains' for clergy in this culture as including status/privilege, power, lack of accountability, and freedom from relational commitments and responsibilities; the 'gains' for laity include the avoidance of responsibility, a clearly defined role, the costs of adult faith, as well as the security and 'reflected glory' that derive from dependence on another.[231]

Given what we know about the mind and actions of the present pope, it does seem that there are solid grounds for hope that the Catholic Church may indeed move towards implementing the more collegial vision of Church outlined in the Second Vatican Council. Francis has stressed the primacy of our encounter in faith with Jesus Christ and the mission which flows from this: this is a foundation which can be shared by all, conservatives and liberals alike. He then indicates why this mission requires synodal reform and has taken substantial moves in this direction, often along the lines suggested by various commentators since the Second Vatican Council. And so, as we have seen, we have the beginnings of curial and CDF reform; the establishment of the collegial Council of Cardinals as an instrument of governance; the increasing delegation of powers to local and regional episcopal conferences; consultation of laity in preparation for important decisions and the encouragement of a synodal, inclusive way of proceeding at all levels of the Church's organisation. All this is of a piece with his past immersion in the dialogical culture of religious life and its governance,[232] his formation in Ignatian discernment, and his frequent condemnation of clericalism.

230 Pope Francis, Address at Commemorative Ceremony for the Fiftieth Anniversary of the Synod of Bishops, October 2015.
231 Brendan Callaghan, 'On Scandal and scandals: the psychology of clerical paedophilia', Studies, 99, autumn 2010, 343–56, at 351.
232 See Colleen Mary Mallon OP, 'Gracious Resistance, Religious Women Charting an Ecclesial Path', in R. Gaillaredtz (ed.), When the Magisterium Intervenes, Collegeville, MN: Liturgical Press, 2012, 63–85.

It remains the case that there are great advantages to the universal Petrine ministry, not least in our globalised world when leadership is badly needed and when diversity so easily collapses into fragmentation without unity. Ladislas Orsy has spoken about the need '… to search for better balances without damaging vital forces'.[233] It will not be easy to let go of the habits of passive dependence on exclusively Vatican/papal initiatives, not easy to find ways of combining local and regional decision-making with respect for universal authority. The Catholic Church, as Francis acknowledges, will be helped by the experience of other Christian Churches, and perhaps, in time, it can help them with its own experience of a reformed and reimagined papal office, servant of unity, presiding in love.

What kind of leadership? [234]
It remains to examine a little more closely what kind of leadership is involved in this transformation of ecclesial governance to a more synodal mode. One way of approaching an answer is to return to the issue of leadership and freedom of speech.

A part of the answer to the question of leadership is contained in Gabriel Daly's justified polemic against authoritarianism in the Catholic Church in which, as a liberal, he decries the Church's failure to appreciate the vitally enriching importance of theological diversity.[235] It is clear, as Daly himself acknowledges, that under Francis this situation is already changing, and a much more open culture of honest debate is now being encouraged, essential to the proper contribution to Church life of the theological community and the *sense of the faithful*.[236] It is way past time that a punitive reaction to diversity is overcome and time, too, for those who have suffered under this kind of regime to be reintegrated into the fullness of ecclesial life. Daly himself admits that there are limits to diversity, noting that '… everything depends on how

233 Orsy, op. cit., 2009, 12.
234 For what follows see Gerry O'Hanlon, 'Emerging Issues in Catholic Church Reform', *Doctrine and Life*, 66, July–August 2016, 3–15.
235 Gabriel Daly OSA, *The Church, Always in Need of Reform*, Dublin: Dominican Publications, 2015, 8.
236 Gerry O'Hanlon, 'Free Speech in the Church', *Studies*, 105, summer 2016, 199–211.

narrowly or generously the limits are drawn'.[237]

However, is the liberal solution of freedom of speech enough on its own? And is it correct to maintain that there is a radical division of attitudes, an intractable battle, between liberal and conservative Catholics such that there is no possibility of consensus between these mutually contradictory positions?[238] Leadership surely must also include the ability to lay the ground for a changed shared consensus, when a new reading of the signs of the times demands it, and then to take new decisions with reasonable hope of maintaining unity?

Have there not been many instances of a changed consensus resulting in different decisions within the Catholic Church (think of slavery, religious freedom and nowadays the equality of women and the growing convergence in inter-Church ecumenical statements, not to mention the 'anomalies' around ministry already referred to above) and in wider society too (think in our own times of the Northern Ireland situation, of civil rights in the United States, of apartheid in South Africa), where previously supposedly intractable oppositions were overcome? Does classical liberalism accept sufficiently the challenge – after all the necessary talking – of taking decisions for the common good in situations that continue to be contested? Does its hermeneutic of suspicion towards authority allow it to imagine the intrinsically positive potentialities of leadership? In a review of Daly's book ecclesiologist Richard Gaillardetz's question is worth pondering: 'But does not a commitment to the catholicity of the Church require a third option beyond a suppression of disagreement on the one hand, and a reluctant tolerance of a diversity of views on the other?'[239]

Leadership – power, authority, community
Elsewhere, in a more extended theological reflection,[240] Gaillardetz analyses power and authority in the Church in a way that helps to appreciate the complexities and positive potentialities of leadership and how these might bear on the current situation.

---

237 Gabriel Daly, 'Difference, Division and the Acceptance of Diversity', Address to We are the Church reform group, 15 January 2018.
238 Daly, op. cit., 10.
239 R. Gaillardetz, *The Tablet*, 30 April 2016, 18.
240 Richard R. Gaillardetz, 'Power and Authority in the Church: Emerging Issues', in Gaillardetz and Hahnenberg (eds), op. cit., 87–111.

With regard to power, Gaillardetz draws first on Weber's notion that power is associated with the ability of an actor or group of actors to carry out their will within a given set of social relationships.[241] It does not presuppose consent, whereas authority does. Weber's is a predominantly zero-sum understanding of power, characterised by domination and coercion. This has led some Christians to accept his general account of power but then to call for a Christian repudiation of power in imitation of the powerlessness of Christ. Gaillardetz argues that this is too simplistic, that one of the most distinctive features of Jesus' ministry was his exercise of power as a manifestation of the love of God, vulnerable and yet liberating.[242] This is a power which subverts the habits of worldly power and domination in favour of humble service and reconciliation, a power which is transformed, redeemed, which empowers.

How might we conceptualise the kind of ecclesial reform that could bring about this redemption of power?[243] This time Gaillardetz draws on Foucault's notion that power is a reality that inheres within all relational networks, that it is not simply a question of a zero-sum game (with its focus on the state), but only one of how power is 'disciplined' within particular 'technologies' or mechanisms of power. In the ecclesial context Gaillardetz argues that our analysis of power has been too limited to juridical power regulated by canon law – without ignoring this, we must recover that more comprehensive dimension of ecclesial power that comes from baptism and is animated by the Spirit. The disciplining of power proper to Christian discipleship will involve more than a simple redistribution of (coercive) power to pastoral councils, but will, instead, bring about a transformation of the way that all power is conceived and exercised.

Gaillardetz then explores some of the habits that need to be cultivated in order to transform power from the habits of domination to those in accord with the values of God's reign. He notes in particular the need for the teaching Church to first become a learning Church in which the teaching ministry of the bishops is

241 Ibid., 89.
242 Ibid., 88–90.
243 Ibid., 90–102.

located within the community of the baptised and the contribution of the *sensus fidei* is cultivated and respected. The 'sense of the faithful' serves not only, through the process of 'reception', as a touchstone for the authenticity of Church teaching, but, sharing in the prophetic office of Jesus Christ, serves also (with theologians and bishops) as one of the threefold sources of Church teaching. In this context of 'disciplined power' bishops will exercise their teaching responsibilities through prayer, study, consultation and dialogue, and not presume that teaching is merely an exercise in governance to which the appropriate response is obedience and not also understanding.

Gaillardetz goes on to discuss[244] how this notion of power relates to notions of authority (the qualification of a set of ecclesial relationships in which individuals or communities freely consent to participate in the exercise of power as both agents and recipients[245]). He begins by noting the prevailing hermeneutic of suspicion with regard to authority, an unfortunate by-product of the Enlightenment and with roots also in Freud, Marx and Nietzsche. He argues that ultimately authority is in the service of human flourishing and the common good, it is central to our existence as relational beings living in community. He draws on the distinction by Victor Lee Austin between substitutory (parents, for example) and non-substitutory (the conductor of an orchestra, for example) forms of authority. The latter, a more mature form of authority, functions so as to coordinate individual human activity for the sake of corporate action. Authority, in this sense, enables the exercise of freedom to serve the life of communion, of the community – in the words of John Courtney Murray, 'self-fulfilment is the achievement of freedom for communion with others'.[246]

Another way of putting this is to say that authority serves the common good. What is at stake here is a recognition that, at its best, authority is not a necessary evil, imposed from outside (or from 'above'), but is linked to our identity as human beings who are intrinsically relational and live in community. Without the power

244 Ibid., 102–110.
245 Ibid., 88.
246 Ibid., 104.

of authority the richness of our differences as individuals risks descending into communal chaos. Speaking about authority and community Ladislas Orsy[247] has similarly argued that

In a healthy community the two are organically united; one cannot have one without the other. Authority is the central organ of community; its task is to create and to maintain unity in the group. Authority is not added to the community from the outside; it is a necessary creation from the inside. Nor it is opposed to community: it is an integral part of it.[248]

Gaillardetz concludes his reflections by noting the excessive reliance on a juridical model of legitimisation of authority in ecclesial circles, in particular among clergy. He notes the need, articulated by Joseph Komonchak, for 'trustworthy' and not just 'legitimate' power if a deeper climate of consent to authority is to be rediscovered in the Church. Trustworthiness will include good will (a commitment to act in support of the common good), competency (at least at a basic level, otherwise the authority of office suffers) and accountability (not just to those above office-holders, but to all the baptised). It will help, in this context, when mistakes are made (as is inevitable) that they are admitted – Francis, who has described himself as a sinner (Interview), gave leadership here in admitting that his words about the sexual abuse controversy in Chile during his visit there in January 2018 were ill-chosen, and caused survivors of abuse offence and hurt, for which he asked their forgiveness.

The Church Today

We have seen how a more synodal Church poses significant challenges to Church leadership today. Gabriel Daly's critique, arguing for freedom of speech, is very much at one with Gaillardetz's judgement that 'since the eighteenth century the Catholic Church has relied on a naive sacralisation of power and authority that has enabled significant abuse'.[249] However, freedom of speech is not only an end it itself. At its best it is also a contribution to that often

---

247 Ladislas Orsy, *Probing the Spirit, A Theological Evaluation of Communal Discernment,* New Jersey: Dimension Books, 1976.
248 Ibid., 70.
249 Gaillardetz, op. cit., 110.

conflicted discernment of the common good in which Spirit-led communities must always engage if they are to read the signs of the times.

With this in mind, Gaillardetz has argued for a 'disciplined', transformed power within the Church, in imitation of the Jesus who came not to be served but to serve and who did so in situations of resistance and conflict. This will mean that the Church, as a 'school' for Christian discipleship, animated by the Holy Spirit, cultivates appropriate habits of power and practices of communal discernment,[250] exercised within a network of authority relationships that order and enhance the freedom of believers and empower the Church for its mission. What, in the concrete, might this imply for Church leadership today?

I think it means, firstly, a broadening and deepening of the synodal process in the Church. Francis, as noted, has spoken often of a key principle of change summed up in the maxim that 'time is greater than space' (especially EG, 222–25). By this he means to stress the importance of initiating processes towards significant historical change rather than focusing on short-term, immediate results. This is precisely what the shift towards a synodal Church is designed to do – change now occurs not through a papal or Vatican fiat but in the context of a genuine dialogue, respecting the roles of bishops, theologians and faithful in their contributions to authentic teaching and governance. If he can succeed in coaxing the Church in this direction, then, not only will he have laid the foundations for a better way of exercising power, authority and Magisterium in the Church but also for a culture and approach that can outlive his own pontificate.

Secondly, Francis himself knows well that this is slow work (EG, 223) and that the fruits are gradual (see the real but modest results of the synods on the family). What he has done very well, as noted, is to cultivate attitudes in the Church which are favourable to this new approach, to risk experimenting with a more dynamic synodal model, to encourage bishops and others worldwide to do the same

250 Gerry O'Hanlon, 'Discernment and the Synod on the Family', *Doctrine and Life*, 65, September 2015, 9–20.

(maintaining that synodality is what 'God expects from the Church in the third millennium', that 'church and synod are synonymous' and that synodality extends to all levels of Church life).[251] In this he is true to his own conviction that a change of attitude or culture has a certain priority over structural or institutional reform.[252]

One can see the logic of this approach – recall how Gaillardetz stressed the need for transformed power and not simply a redistribution of the secular model of coercive and dominating power. However, as Francis has also indicated, structural and legal reform is also important and we do well to remember one of the key lessons from the relative failure to implement the Second Vatican Council more fully – there was ample cultural and theological change then, but the lack of structural and juridical change resulted in the failure to ground collegiality and synodality in particular in the institutional organisation of the Church.[253] Might it soon be time for Francis to legislate for the more regular occurrence of synods in Church life, to introduce a deliberative and not just consultative model of synodality, 'with and under Peter' and to amend Canon 129 of the Revised Code of Canon Law in order to assert the right of laity to decision-making powers in the Church (see Chapter Nine)? Thirdly, there is an invitation to all the baptised faithful to be part of this new synodal model of Church as a way of exercising responsible discipleship. It cannot happen without 'buy-in' from the faithful – this will mean leadership from bishops and priests, but also the willingness of laity to claim their baptismal authority. Chapter Eight will discuss this and the contested issue of the role of women in the Church in particular.

251 Gerry O'Hanlon, 'The Quiet Revolution – Reflections on Synod 2015', *The Furrow*, 66, December 2015, 632–41.
252 'The structural and organisational reforms are secondary ... the first reform must be attitude' – Pope Francis, in interview with Antonio Spadaro SJ, September 2013.
253 John W. O'Malley, *What Happened at Vatican II,* Harvard, MA: Harvard University Press, 2008, 311–12.

CHAPTER EIGHT

The Role of Laity, including Women, in Authority

But we need to create still broader opportunities for a more incisive female presence in the Church. (EG, 103)

The transition towards a synodal Church raises questions around the participation of lay people in Church governance. In particular there is an urgent and serious question about the exercise of authority by women in the Catholic Church, a question shared by Pope Francis.[254]

Church, Women, Authority: Why Not?
I want to begin my reflections on this question from what may seem a round-about starting point but is in fact the centre from which all else flows. Francis does this himself by noting that 'the most important thing', the 'first proclamation', is 'that Jesus Christ has saved you' (Interview), it is 'the beauty of the saving love of God made manifest in Jesus Christ' (EG, 36), so that 'mercy is the greatest of all the virtues' (EG,37) and 'Jesus Christ is the face of the Father's mercy'(Bull of Indiction for the Year of Mercy, 2015). This is the mystery at the heart of the Christian faith, the joy of the Gospel, good news for all men and women – God as Trinity, as love, wanting to share this love with us, who are good but are also vulnerable and sinners. It is from this basic starting point of enormous gratitude, in response to the mystery of God's love encountered in faith through Jesus Christ, that we worship, but also

---

254 For what follows see O'Hanlon, 'Church, Women, Authority – *Why Not?*', *Doctrine and Life*, 66, January 2016, 23–32.

that we question and theologise – faith, as Anselm put it, seeking understanding.

Since the Church is meant to mirror, to reveal this love of God, the Kingdom of God, it is right that we are disturbed, even angry, when it seems that in its practice the Church has become in this matter of authority and women an anti-sign, instead of a sacrament, of God's love. However, the questioning, the disturbance, the anger, the campaigning for justice are better located when they emerge from a deep appreciation of God's love – otherwise they run the danger of losing touch with their roots and becoming arid and self-consuming.

The disturbance is clearly shared by Pope Francis. He has spoken about the need to broaden the opportunities for a stronger presence of women in the Church, stating that 'the feminine genius is needed wherever we make important decisions' and that the 'challenge today is this: to think about the specific place of women in those places where the authority of the Church is exercised for various areas of the church' and to 'work harder to develop a profound theology of woman' (Interview). In *Evangelii Gaudium* he speaks of the need for 'a more incisive female presence in the Church', stating that the presence of women must be guaranteed 'where important decisions are made, both in the Church and in social structures' (EG, 103), and that this presents the Church 'with profound and challenging questions which cannot be lightly evaded' (EG, 104).

In facing this challenge Francis gives a hint of how to proceed: not, for him, by way of ordination (not open for discussion – EG, 104), but rather by distinguishing between sacramental power and power in general. He seems to be hinting here that there is too close an identification between the sacrament of Orders and jurisdiction on the one hand and power in general on the other, and that we ought to look to the dignity conferred by Baptism as a basis for a more just participation in power and authority by lay women and men alike (EG, 102–4).

Sacred Power and the Laity
An historical perspective is helpful in this matter – as indeed in so many disputed issues: we sometimes imagine that because things

are so they have always been so and must be so. This was the great discovery of the Second Vatican Council in their *ressourcement* approach: by going back to the sources they discovered that things could be and were sometimes different than they now are.

In this context, the eminent canon lawyer and theologian Ladislas Orsy is most helpful.[255] He notes that the ecumenical councils of the first millennium, called by the Byzantine emperors and empresses, were surely acts of jurisdiction by laymen and laywomen. The majority of participants at the Council of Florence were not 'in orders', therefore 'lay votes' had a real impact on the determinations concerning the reunion of the Eastern and Western Churches. Abbesses for centuries exercised 'quasi-episcopal jurisdiction' in governing 'quasi-dioceses' – except in dispensing sacraments, for which ordination was necessary. Such 'lay prelates' had 'the power of jurisdiction', with the full and direct support of the Holy See, well into the nineteenth century.[256] In short, the historical evidence for lay people participating in decision-making processes in the Church is over-whelming, from at least the fourth century and well into the twentieth century.

Of course that is not the situation today. Orsy describes it thus:

In the beginning of this twenty-first century we live in the middle of a paradox – and the faithful are hardly aware of it. On the one hand, the pronouncements of Vatican II brought remarkable results and opened the door for an increased promotion of the laity. On the other hand, the official policy of the church based on a recent theological opinion that found its way into the revised code of canon law excludes the laity from any *major* decision-making processes – reversing an immemorial tradition.[257]

What has happened is that a theological opinion about 'the sacred power', not sufficiently debated by theologians, has become standard and has been incorporated into the Revised Code of Canon

255 See Ladislas Orsy, 'Discourse about the Laity', in *Receiving the Council*, Collegeville, MN: Liturgical Press, 2009, 35–45; and 'Lay persons in church governance?: A disputed question', *America*, 6 April 1996.
256 Ibid., 39.
257 Ibid., 35–36.

Law (1983), in particular in Canon 129. This canon specifies that those who have received sacred orders are qualified for the power of governance, also called the power of jurisdiction; lay members of the Christian faithful can cooperate in the exercise of this same power. The words are carefully chosen: cooperate is not the same as participate, and means in effect that lay persons are excluded from significant decision-making processes, that no lay person is admitted 'into the inner sanctuary' that is to have a significant role in building the Church from within where ecclesiastical 'jurisdiction' is in play. Consultation yes, deliberation no. Orsy, who is careful with words, says that the exclusion of laity from participation in government is 'a novelty and an unwarranted ideology'.[258]

This trend was already apparent in the first part of the twentieth century after the First Vatican Council, and led Pius XI to issue his famous statement in 1939 concerning the overly-clerical disfigurement of the Church as the Body of Christ. It is at the heart of the problem of clericalism which Pope Francis has clearly identified as a blight on the Church.

If the challenge of Francis is to be met – to imagine a role for lay people, and in particular women, in the decision-making processes of the Church – then Canon 129 has to be removed and we have to return theologically to the understanding of Baptism outlined in *Lumen Gentium*, which referred to Church as the People of God. Through Baptism each of these people – lay and cleric alike – receives a share in the threefold office of Jesus Christ as prophet, priest and king (LG, 31). There is no historical precedent, as we have seen, for limiting this power of governance in the manner that has become common practice today.

What might happen if this challenge were met and the necessary theological and canonical work done? Well, it would seem that lay people (including, of course, women) could be voting members of synods or councils; full members of decision-making bodies in the ordinary administration of the Church – for example Roman congregations and offices; in charge of the assets of the Church; duly qualified lay preachers of the word – all on the basis of the

258 Orsy, *America*, 1996.

sacred power given to every Christian through Baptism.

I simply note by way of conclusion to this point that decision-making needs to change at all levels of the Church. It is true that the role of laity is constrained by Canon 129 – and so, for example, parish councils are only advisory and consultative, not deliberative. But diocesan councils, assemblies and even synods are also predominantly consultative – the bishop retains sovereignty. And then, at a higher level, the Synod of Bishops, as presently constituted, is purely consultative, so that, technically, the pope may decide on his own. Only ecumenical councils – with and under the pope – have decision-making powers. In practice this change is beginning to happen. Francis has made it clear that he wants open debate, real and not just token consultation, the 'sense of the faithful' to be attended to, a more dynamic Synod of Bishops which has real power. But all this, at this point, is discretionary and is not the law of the Church – for it to be sustainable and flourish (also after the present pontificate) it requires appropriate theological and legal underpinning.

Why is any of this important? Because we have seen the terrible consequences of exclusively clerical power, and we know that it is a great loss – a sinful omission in fact – not to involve the wisdom of the wider People of God in the decision-making as well as the formation of teaching in our Church. The observation of Orsy in this context is helpful: 'The numerous cases of abuse of minors have revealed an organisation that lacks a vigorous "immune system" for self-protection; an infection can spread in the body before it is noticed and remedial action can be taken.'[259]

The Question of Ordination

We are faced with a strange situation concerning the issue of ordination. While the Church continues to insist that women can't be ordained, many ordinary people (including members of the Catholic faithful) genuinely fail to make sense of the reasons for this position. Given this difficulty around credibility it may be helpful to take another look at the Church's stance.

259 Orsy, op. cit., 2009, 2.

The principal document outlining the Church's teaching on the ordination of women, *Inter Insigniores,* was published by the Congregation for the Doctrine of the Faith in October 1976. The teaching was reconfirmed by Pope John Paul II in his Apostolic Letter *Ordinatio Sacerdotalis* (OS), May 1994, with the addendum that this was not just a disciplinary matter, open to further debate, but was a 'judgement to be definitively held by all the Church's faithful' (OS, 4).

There has been considerable discussion over the legitimacy of this theological category of 'definitive teaching' (not infallible, but irreformable – what does this mean?) and the accompanying corollary that if one wants to remain a member of the Catholic Church one must simply accept, and not even discuss, the non-ordination of women.[260] Is the doctrine of 'definitive teaching' an instance of legitimate theological development or a theological novelty which will be rejected?[261] And does it apply to the issue of the ordination of women?

Whatever about the outcome of that particular debate, it remains the case that the non-discussability of the issue has been stated by several popes and so, for any responsible Catholic, demands respect. But what does 'not open to discussion' mean? Christopher O'Donnell is most helpful here:[262] he distinguishes, following the tradition, between questions for understanding (*quid sit*) and questions which lead to a yes/no answer (*an sit).* This corresponds well to the distinction that philosopher Bernard Lonergan makes between understanding and judgement in his cognitional theory.[263] Questions for understanding – even about the most solemnly defined Church teachings – are always open for discussion. Thus, O'Donnell argues that while 'one is no longer free to assert boldly that women should be ordained', nonetheless one is always free to examine and

260 See Gerry O'Hanlon, 'Free Speech in the Church', *Studies,* 105, summer 2016, 199–2011, at 204-6.
261 For a fuller discussion, in dialogue with Cardinal Ratzinger, then Prefect of the CDG, see Ladislas Orsy, 'Definitive Doctrine and Ordinances Supporting It', in *Receiving the Council,* Collegeville, MN: Liturgical Press, 2009, 115–42.
262 Christopher O'Donnell O Carm, *Ecclesia, A Theological Encyclopedia of the Church,* Collegeville, MN: Liturgical Press, 1996, article on Women, Ordination of, 474–78.
263 Bernard J. F. Lonergan SJ, *Insight, A Study of Human Understanding,* London: Longmans, Green & Co, 1957.

attempt to understand the main arguments given in the matter. I would simply add at this point that if such an examination, over a long time, and with a sufficient consensus emerging, continues to leave many people unconvinced by the reasons given, then, since this is not an infallible teaching, there begins to emerge a strong case for more open discussion of the '*an sit*' question too, the teaching itself.[264] In this context I recall again the salutary remark of the Melkite Patriach Maximos IV Saïgh to Paul VI at the Second Vatican Council: 'repressed truths turn poisonous'.[265] Meanwhile, it is clear that Francis himself, while repeating the veto on the ordination of women, is in practice more relaxed about discussion of the issue, in line with his call for open and honest dialogue in general.

The main argument in both teaching documents is 'that the Church, in fidelity to the example of the Lord, does not consider herself authorised to admit women to priestly ordination' (InterIn, Introduction). This argument is based on the fact that Jesus called only men to be part of the Twelve, that the early apostolic community maintained this 'men only' norm, as did the subsequent tradition down through the ages. The document maintains that the practice of Jesus 'was not in order to conform to the customs of his time, for his attitude towards women was quite different from that of his milieu, and he deliberately and courageously broke with it' (InterIn, 2). Similarly, when the early apostolic community encountered Greco-Roman civilisation with its more liberal attitude to women they could have envisaged conferring ordination on women 'if they had not been convinced of their duty of fidelity to the Lord on this point' (InterIn, 3).

There are substantial points within this argument, presented here only in summary form but developed in greater detail in the two source documents in question as well as in other texts of the Magisterium.[266] However, it is also clear that the argument – from Tradition, based on Scripture – is not without its difficulties. Apart

264 See O'Hanlon, 'Church, Women, Authority, Why Not?', *Doctrine and Life*, 66, January 2016, 23–32.
265 O'Malley, op. cit., 272.
266 See, for example, John Paul II, *Christifideles Laici*, 1988, n. 51; *Mulieris Dignitatem*, 1994, n. 26; Congregation for the Doctrine of the Faith, *Responsum ad Propositum Dubium*, 1995.

from the questionable exclusive identification of priesthood with the Twelve (they were the eschatological foundation of the new people of God, based on the twelve tribes of Israel, not just priests), there is the admission in *Inter Insigniores* itself that 'it is true that these facts do not make matters immediately obvious ... a purely historical exegesis of texts cannot suffice' (InterIn, 2). This admission is more striking when one considers the Report of the Pontifical Biblical Commission in April 1976 (part of which was leaked and published in July 1976), whose membership included such eminent scripture scholars as Raymond Brown and Carlo Martini. Their report, in an unfinished document, recorded the following three votes:

1) A unanimous (17–0) vote that the New Testament does not settle in any clear way and once and for all whether women can be ordained priests

2) A 12–5 vote in favour of the view that scriptural grounds alone are not enough to exclude the possibility of ordaining women and

3) A 12–5 vote that Christ's plan would not be transgressed by permitting the ordination of women

Given that *Inter Insigniores* itself acknowledges that the modern question concerning the ordination of women is posed in a way 'which classical theology scarcely touched upon', and given the admitted lack of clarity around the biblical evidence, is it not strange that the appeal to Tradition can be couched in such absolute terms – 'I declare that the Church has no authority whatsoever to confer priestly ordination on women' (OS, 4)? Further, despite the solemnity of the language in *Ordinatio Sacerdotalis* and its undoubted authoritative weight, theological opinion is clear that we do not have here infallible teaching.[267]

A second argument is advanced in *Inter Insigniores* by way of showing the 'fittingness' (*ex convenientia*/analogy of faith) that theological reflection can discover to support the norm that has been claimed to exist. This argument states that the priest acts not in his own name but '*in persona Christi*' (in the person of Christ), that it is important in the Eucharist and in all the sacraments that the priest be

267 See Christopher O'Donnell O Carm, op. cit., 475; Ladislas Orsy, op. cit., 2009, chapters 8 and 9.

a sign of Christ bearing 'natural resemblance' to him and that 'Christ himself was and remains a man' (n 5). This argument is sometimes developed theologically along the lines of an anthropology of complementarity, which seeks to discern the 'genius of women' to reside in the active receptivity that accompanies love, and to suppose that public leadership is more the domain of men.

Francis himself has advanced this issue in *Amoris Laetitia* by signalling a significant shift in official Church teaching theologising on the role of women, a shift that has the potential for doctrinal development.[268] I am referring here to his clear approval of feminism ('we must see in the women's movement the working of the Spirit' – AL, 54) and, above all, to his more sympathetic attitude towards gender theory and his acceptance that masculinity and femininity are not simply the result of 'biological or genetic factors' but are also influenced by historical and cultural influences and are not 'rigid categories' so that, for example, it is not correct to assert that '… it is not very feminine to exercise leadership' (AL, 286).

The extent of the theological shift involved here is indicated by the analysis of Mary Ann Hinsdale, which identifies 'gender complementarity' as the 'issue under the issues' blocking the proper advancement of the role of women in the Church.[269] She notes that the theory of gender complementarity has assumed official theological status in the Church since, under the influence of the theological poetics of Hans Urs von Balthasar, it was adopted by John Paul II about thirty years ago and expressed most eloquently in his Theology of the Body in particular. It claims that there is an underlying anthropological foundation for masculinity and femininity, a kind of ontological 'given', which is independent of historic-socio-cultural factors, is complementary, and is determinative of appropriate masculine and feminine roles – so, for example, 'femaleness is characterised by receptivity and maternal

268 See Gerry O'Hanlon, 'Emerging Issues in Catholic Church Reform', *Doctrine and Life*, 66, July–August 2016, 3–15, at 6–8.
269 Mary Ann Hinsdale IHM, 'A Feminist Reflection on Postconciliar Catholic Ecclesiology', in Richard R. Gaillardetz and Edward P. Hahnenberg (eds), *A Church with Open Doors, Catholic Ecclesiology for the Third Millennium*, Collegeville, MN: Liturgical Press, 2015, 112–37.

nurturing, while maleness consists of initiation and agency'.[270] It is one of the theological arguments from 'fittingness' that underpins the ban on the ordination of women, with the implication that public leadership roles clash with the predominantly receptive vocation of women. It is opposed to other forms of 'gender theory' which distinguish socially constructed gender roles from biological sex. It is argued by feminists that it undermines the effective equality of Christian discipleship by its insistence that equality does not require identity, thus limiting Church leadership and power to men.

What Francis is signalling here is a certain softening of the Church's official stance against gender theory and 'secular feminism',[271] and an admission that 'gender complementarity' can be read in an excessively essentialist way. In her own reflections Hinsdale had suggested that we needed to get beyond the impasse by entering into a dialogue between the two positions, a discernment which would be an exercise of the 'disciplinary power' (Gaillardetz) proper to Christian discipleship and leadership, and might include the kind of ethnographic study recommended by Hahnenberg[272] as an inductive approach to balance the more deductive methods of the proponents of gender complementarity.

This is what Francis seems to be doing, and this impression is further strengthened by his establishment of a commission to examine the question of deaconesses in the New Testament (and their possibility today), and his admission (in a 'Q and A' session with women religious leaders from the International Union of Superior Generals) that 'I never imagined there was such a disconnect' (in the context of the voice of women being excluded from conversations within the Church).[273] We are, it seems, already in the process towards a changed consensus on the role of women in the Church.

There are, then, serious issues with the Church's argument from fittingness. Are not women also made in the image and likeness of God, who is neither male nor female? Cannot women also be

270 Ibid., 125.
271 Ibid., 128–9.
272 Edward P. Hahnenberg, 'Learning from Experience: Attention to Anomalies in a Theology of Ministry', in Gaillardetz and Hahnenberg, op. cit., 159–80, at 167–70.
273 Cindy Wooden, Catholic News Service, 12 May 2016.

ministers of sacraments (by way of exception in Baptism and quite normally in Matrimony)? A basic principle of soteriology is that 'what has not been assumed has not been saved' – surely the humanity of Christ is more important than his sexuality, since otherwise female sexuality has not been saved, which would be heretical? Are not superiors in women's religious congregations understood to be acting '*in persona Christi*'? And, finally, whatever about the real and pervasive differences between men and women (often denied by those who stress cultural factors only), can they really be described in terms of public leadership, at a time when, in other domains, the Church praises the leadership role of women in public life?

Conclusion
Catholics will want to respect Church teaching, but in doing so they are correct to hope that the reasons underpinning the teaching are persuasive. I have adverted to some questions concerning the reasons given to underpin the Church's present teaching on the ordination of women. This teaching, presented here only in summary form but developed in greater detail in the two principal source documents mentioned and also in other texts of the Magisterium, gives rise to several questions. Might these questions and others (evidence of a difficulty in the 'reception' of the teaching) lead the Magisterium 'to reflect on the teaching that has been given and consider whether it needs clarification or reformulation'?[274] In short, might there be a need for a reconsideration of this issue, availing of all the biblical and theological expertise available, and drawing as well on the 'sense of the faithful'? Might Francis agree to this reconsideration in the light of his plea for a 'more profound theology of woman' (Interview)?

Nonetheless, because the Church has been so vehement in its denial of female ordination, it is arguable that to tackle this issue too directly and immediately would be to threaten unity at a fundamental level. It may be better to encourage the Church authorities to listen more carefully to what its members are saying on the issue.

274 International Theological Commission, '*Sensus Fidei' in the Life of the Church*, 2014, 80.

Sidney Tarrow's analysis is apt here. He has stressed the particular significance of 'political opportunity' (in this case we can refer to the election of Francis as a reforming pope) in the struggle for any justice cause, and the wisdom of arguing for access to input, influence and power when such an opportunity presents itself (in this case the transition to synodality), rather than opting for singular and concrete gains which may be of less lasting significance.[275] It would be helpful on this issue to open up as quickly as possible the ministry of diaconate for women. Bishop Leo O'Reilly has already called for this in response to a listening exercise in the Kilmore Diocese. Apart from being less threatening to ecclesial unity, this move would have the merit of testing the waters, allowing the 'sense of the faithful' to discern the aptness of this development of public ministry for women, and the Magisterium, accordingly, to read the 'signs of the times'. More recently, it is interesting that the vice-president of the German Bishops' Conference, Bishop Franz-Josef Bode of Osnabrück, has called for the Vatican commission on the diaconate for women to expand its work on leadership roles for women in the Church, noting that '… this question will ultimately have to be decided by a council or synod'.[276]

It will also help in this context to acknowledge again that historically Tradition has developed and changed, often due to the 'sense of the faithful'. In particular if we attend to the verse in Galatians 3, 28: 'There is neither Jew nor Greek, there is neither slave nor free, there is neither male nor female', we can observe that the mind of Jesus on these matters was not so obvious to the early Church as to prevent, already within the New Testament corpus itself, a conflict about how to resolve the matter of Jews and Gentiles; that it took the best part of two millennia to sort out the Christian stance on slavery; and that, clearly, we are still in the throes of confronting the gender issue. Might the change of argument from the inferiority of women to their complementarity (understood to preclude their ordination) mask an ongoing misogyny and patriarchy, however unconscious?

However, there need be no delay or hesitation about following

275 Sidney G. Tarrow, *Power in Movement, Social Movements and Contentious Politics,*
    Cambridge: Cambridge University Press, 2011, 159–67.
276 *America,* 12 January 2018.

up on the challenge posed by Francis himself in envisaging a more visible and authoritative role for laity in general and women in particular in our Church, apart altogether from the question of Orders. This was a central theme of the much-noticed 'empire of misogyny' speech delivered by Mary McAleese at the Voices of Faith International Women's Day Conference at Jesuit headquarters in Rome on 8 March 2018. I have indicated the lines along which we can proceed in this issue, and not to do so would be unconscionable. The need to so proceed became even more apparent after the Synod on the Family in which there were no voting women participants, while, anomalously, one non-ordained man (a religious brother) did have voting rights.

Francis himself may at times reveal, to western ears, a rather quaint and even grating image of women in some of what he says. What is important however is his recognition of the problem, and, more significantly still, his opening up of the Church to debate, real consultation, respect for the 'sense of the faithful', a collegial approach to teaching so that bishops are 'to listen to everyone and not simply to those who would tell him what he likes to hear' (EG, 31). This is surely the most hopeful sign for the future, a sign which can outlive the pontificate of Francis himself: a way of proceeding in a synodal model of Church that is intent on listening to the promptings of the Holy Spirit through the voices of the faithful and which creates the appropriate structures and institutions to allow this to happen.[277] In this way we can hope that the questioning and often just anger, the 'lamentations' of Hinze, to which issues like the role of women in the Church give rise, may be handled in such a way that they are a clear manifestation of the ever-greater love of God and our grateful response.

---

277 Gerry O'Hanlon, 'The Quiet Revolution – Reflections on Synod 2015', *The Furrow,* 66, December 2015, 632–41.

PART FOUR

Ireland Revisited

CHAPTER NINE

Synodality and the Catholic Church in Ireland

And it is precisely on this way of synodality where we find the pathway that God expects from the Church of the third millennium.
(Pope Francis, Address at Commemorative Ceremony for the Fiftieth Anniversary of the Synod of Bishops, 2015)

We have seen how Pope Francis is trying to reposition the Catholic Church in the modern world. He is doing so in response to many serious challenges. There is, culturally, the rise of secularisation, in the western world in particular. Economically there has emerged the dominance of a particular paradigm of economic theory, which deepens inequality and environmental damage and threatens to colonise all our thinking. Within the Church itself there is a clear need to develop a healthy immune system to counter the terrible crimes of clerical child sexual abuse, to deal with Vatican finances, and to tackle the systemic culture of clericalism, with its casual assumption of the rights of one class of Christian to be considered superior, and therefore fit to govern and to constitute the teaching Church on its own.

We have seen how Francis is basing this reimagination of Catholicism on the biblical revelation of our encounter with Jesus Christ in faith. This will mean less an exclusive prominence given to the quasi-certainty accorded to loyal repetition of the 'deposit of faith', and more a trusting commitment to the vulnerability of relationship. When we fall in love and grow into a relationship, we are all too conscious of not being able to categorise or control the mystery of another person – and this is infinitely more so when that other is God. In this context Francis often speaks of the need to respect and nourish tenderness, an inherently vulnerable quality: the heart of our faith, as the Second Vatican Council pointed out, is the living encounter with the person of Jesus Christ, not the certainty of propositional truths. And, yes, doctrine and even dogma will arise from this encounter, it will be possible to develop life-giving theologies and write helpful catechisms, but without the sense of relationship at its core all is so much 'straw', as Aquinas memorably said.

We have seen how, given the culture of today and our own more collegial past in Scripture and Tradition, Francis is proposing a synodal model of Church as a response to contemporary challenges. This will involve, among other things, a more inclusive role for lay men and women in Church teaching and governance. I have argued that his is an appropriate response. As is normal, given the scale of the revolution he is proposing and the human propensity to prefer even a dubious stability and certainty to what is perceived as an unfamiliar and risky change, there is considerable opposition to his proposal, an opposition that intensifies as progress in implementation of change becomes evident.

It is hardly conceivable that Francis's project can be successful without being accepted and implemented by the rest of the Church: decentralisation will not occur if the regions and peripheries do not want, or are not able, to accept more responsibility, and cultural Catholicism will remain the norm if more people are not attracted and willing to accept the baptismal invitation to be intentional disciples, to grow in that relationship with Jesus Christ.

We in Ireland have particular reason to respond with serious consideration to the project of Francis. Faith does not simply disappear overnight, and there are continuing signs of spiritual vitality in our country. But the institutional presence needed to support this faith in the longer run can no longer be taken for granted. The moral authority of the Catholic Church has been severely damaged and there is a clear crisis of priestly vocations, the inroads of secularisation have deepened, and there is a loss of meaning in our society due not least to the pre-eminence of an economic model that threatens to dominate the whole of life. How are we in Ireland doing in response to the project of Francis, what are the points of resistance and growth?

Here I draw on the analysis already outlined (particularly in Chapter Two), but also on the privileged experience of having travelled the length and breadth of Ireland over the last ten years in response to invitations to speak at gatherings of parishes, and of priests and bishops.

The Irish response: challenges, opportunities, obstacles

I turn first to the challenges facing the realisation of a synodal Church in Ireland, that 'new, more culturally appropriate constellation' which Michael Conway advocated for our Irish situation.

At the parish level Irish theologian Jim Corkery outlines a synodal vision of this more appropriate constellation which many parishes are trying to implement.[278] This includes: the priest at the centre of parish life, but not at its apex; a less male-centred community; a space for people to speak, to be listened to, and, in particular, a reaching out in this respect to young people and those who have been alienated; a sense of learning from, as well as teaching to, 'the world', a kind of 'dynamic mutuality' in which we recall that the Church is both *docens* and *discerns* (learning and teaching); developing a new culture with significantly changed relationships in which authority would be shared.

In practice Corkery speaks of homily-preparation in dialogue with different groups of parishioners; financial and temporal management only tangentially the priest's concern; a kind of 'permanent council' (members rotating) with much more 'teeth' than a controlled parish council that a priest can override and which can deliberate and plan; and teams helping in ministries such as marriage and baptism preparation, instruction in faith, adult education and training, liturgical preparation, service to the poor and so on; and, given the shortage of priests, 'reflection on how to provide for sacramental

278 See Jim Corkery SJ, "'Our Own Hope Had Been" … (Lk 24:21): The Promise of Vatican II – Reality or Illusion?', in Dr Suzanne Mulligan (ed.), *Reaping the Harvest: Fifty Years after Vatican II*, Dublin: Columba Press, 2012, 13–37, at 32–36.

ministry in new ways (permanent deacons, ordaining mature men as priests, including women in ministry in ways hitherto unimagined) will have to be seriously undertaken'.[279] In this context one could envisage, for example, the clustering of parishes less as a solution to current problems around ordained priesthood and more as the pooling of resources for joint formation of laity leading to more active ministerial participation in church. For all this to happen more effectively there would need to be systematic lay formation and a training for candidates to the priesthood which stressed the service nature of the role and provided them with the skills required for working collaboratively with others.

There is an immediate pastoral challenge implied in this programme, and one that has to be rooted in a mature faith. Eugene Duffy addresses this issue along the lines of a more intense focus on the Church as a 'school of prayer and discernment', offering helpful ways (such as retreat houses, spiritual direction and accompaniment, *lectio divina* groups and so on) 'in which people can begin to discover the desire of God at work today, to discover the love of God in their lives' with the prospect of achieving a 'level of inner peace and freedom that the secular alternatives can never give'.[280] I would add that, as outlined in Chapter Six, this must include induction in the ways of communal discernment, so vital to a synodal Church.

There is also an intellectual challenge involved in facilitating the kind of faith encounter with Jesus Christ which transformed so many lives according to the Gospel narratives, in the modern context of secularisation which seems so inhospitable to religion.[281] Dermot Lane is clear about the challenge involved.[282] Drawing principally on the analysis of Charles Taylor, Lane notes that the process of secularisation is now well advanced in Ireland and goes on to indicate some of the intellectual resources available to Christianity

279 Ibid., 35.
280 See Eugene Duffy, 'Reimagining the Church in Ireland in the Light of Vatican II', in Niall Coll (ed.), *Ireland and Vatican II*, Dublin: Columba Press, 2015, 113–29, at 116.
281 See Gerry O'Hanlon, 'The Catholic Church in Ireland Today', *Studies*, 106, spring 2017, 9–19, at 14–16; D. Vincent Twomey SVD, 'The End of Irish Catholicism? Fifteen Years On', *Studies*, 106, spring 2017, 39–48.
282 Dermot Lane, *Catholic Education in the Light of Vatican II and Laudato Si'*, Dublin: Veritas, 2015.

and Catholicism in facing into this dominant culture – for example, a reconstruction of anthropology along the lines of the human as relational, dialogic, embodied and linguistic, no longer living in an anthropocentric universe. It will be part of the mission of the Irish Church of the future to take seriously the intellectual and educational challenge involved in the development and communication of a new language of faith more attuned to modern ears, and perhaps the increased emergence of theology in the setting of the university is a hopeful sign here.

It is true, of course, that for some – perhaps for many young people in particular – the breakthrough concerning the radical importance of a life of faith and that encounter with Jesus which inspires it may not, in the first instance, be brought about by direct experiences of prayer or intellectual formation. This may occur, instead, through the kind of social idealism which is so characteristic of younger people and which is central to the mission of the Church in its preaching of the Kingdom. There has been a particular resonance between the words and practice of Pope Francis and many young people throughout the world and in Ireland – 'a poor Church for the poor', the centrality of ecology to issues of poverty – all this young people 'get'. The challenge then is to create spaces in which they may begin to explore that side of things together with what they find more difficult in our secularised culture – the link with the full mystery of the person of Jesus Christ, more than just a human exemplar but the image of the Father and the gate into a world of transcendence that, deep down, they experience a yearning for. This kind of approach, again, has already been adumbrated by, among others, Rahner in his notion of mystagogy – a way of uncovering, through dialogue and conversation, the deeper layers of common human experiences and the presence of the Holy Spirit in life experiences such as happiness, success, joy, suffering, illness, bereavement and death, as well as human history and our struggling planet.

Some of this is going on already within the Irish Church for younger people – one thinks of somewhat unique events like pilgrimages, World Youth Day, Taizé visits – and more ordinary everyday features such as gospel choir masses and peer retreats (like the *Kairos* retreat used in some Irish schools). Similarly, for older people there are some opportunities for a deepening of their prayer and faith lives. And for all there are sites and examples of action and witness – think of the St Vincent de Paul Society, Crosscare, Trócaire and so many prophetic individuals. There is also the kind of public prayer and worship which can also be of assistance to secular society, not least with regard to rites of passage and times of celebration and grieving – as well as providing a contemplative antidote to addictive over-activity.

However, progress is patchy, and there is still something missing, something crucial, because the overall feeling is one of fighting a losing uphill battle, of mediocrity. It must be admitted that many older priests, with diminishing energy, find it difficult to change old habits and learn to work more collaboratively with lay people in parishes; that current canon law provisions (among them Canon 129) allow priests an easy 'opt-out' in stressing the discretionary nature of consultation; that many young priests are not inclined to adopt this more collegial model of priesthood; that many of the third-level pastoral and theological centres required to provide the necessary lay formation have folded up or are under pressure; and that many young adults continue to 'grow out' of the Church, as our greying congregations so graphically testify.

Given the vision, the good will and partial successes, but given also the ongoing obstacles and uphill nature of the struggle, how might the organisation of the Catholic Church in Ireland be transformed in such a way that it might come more alive spiritually, in creative fidelity to its foundational faith in Jesus Christ, so that its missionary impact might be culturally relevant, addressing issues like secularisation, socio-economic issues and inequality in a way that Pope Francis clearly envisages? This, we must recall again and again in any talk about organisational restructuring, is the Jesus Christ who 'emptied himself', who looks at the world from the optic of the marginalised and victims, so that a synodal Church will be soulless without a deep relationship with Jesus Christ and his preferential option for the poor, for the peripheries.

Leadership towards the synodal revolution

The thesis of this book has been that the missing link in our response to date in Ireland has been our failure to take on board Francis's proposal for an explicitly synodal Church at all levels, always in the context of a faith relationship with Jesus Christ and a concomitant commitment to his mission. Why not, as argued, put this clearly as the visionary, strategic way forward, encourage parishes and dioceses to develop appropriate cultures and institutions (including gatherings, assemblies and synods), and put this in a context where we plan a series of national assemblies or synods to address together the challenges facing the Irish Church? For this good leadership is required – not just from bishops, but (in response to our baptismal calling), from all the faithful – laity, priests and religious.

Leadership by Bishops

Clearly the role of bishops is crucial. It is not an easy role in today's crisis situation. Some bishops have been formed and educated to govern in a more stable, compliant culture, a culture in which obedience and autonomy were taken for granted. All bishops, up to recently, have been formed in a context where dialogue with contemporary culture was not regarded as such a major priority and where deferential reliance on Rome was a default position which tended to discourage independent, critical thinking. It is a big leap to exercise leadership in a more imaginative and collaborative way, whether within a diocese or between dioceses in the Episcopal Conference. And it is not so easy to distinguish the seemingly endless administrative and pastoral demands on the time and energy of a bishop from the even more important need for vision and strategy at a time of ecclesial crisis.

I recall Gaillardetz's notion of 'disciplined power', with a gospel focus not so much on the juridical nature of legitimate power but more on trustworthiness of power, with expectations of good will, competency, accountability and ability to admit errors. And so, although it will not be easy, the faithful have a right to expect good governance and leadership from individual bishops and from the episcopal conference. One sometimes gets the impression from informal conversation with bishops themselves that they recognise that the episcopal conference itself is weak and almost dysfunctional, and that the real power still lies with individual bishops and dioceses – this is surely an unacceptable interpretation of subsidiarity at a time when synodality is being stressed and when corporate leadership is so vital for our time of crisis.

Some of what is required has already happened or been promised, an encouraging foundation. As well as activity on the ground in parishes, there have already been a number of 'listening' exercises conducted by different dioceses within Ireland, including Down and Connor, Armagh, Kerry, Killaloe, Kilmore (out of which Bishop Leo O'Reilly brought proposals around married priests and female deacons to the Irish Episcopal Conference in June 2015), and, more recently, Killala.[283] In 2016 there was a synod in the Diocese of Limerick, well prepared over an eighteen-month period, with a clear sense of renewal and hope as part of its outcome.[284]

We need to pursue this path more systematically and with greater conviction – and bishops as well as faithful need to come to the point where they see consultation as real and not just token, capable of tackling neuralgic issues, reaching out to the young and disaffected and not just to the already committed who tend to come from a predominantly middle-aged and older demographic. We need also, urgently, to find ways of giving expression in the Irish Catholic Church to the desire of Francis that women exercise leadership roles in the Church.[285]

A case in point with regard to real consultation is the response by the Irish Episcopal Conference to the consultation in 2014 prior to the Synod on the Family in Rome.[286] The conference issued a very interesting statement in the aftermath of the response by 'thousands of people' to the questionnaire from the Synod of Bishops on the

---

283 Brendan Hoban, *The Western People*, 29 January 2018.
284 See Eamonn Fitzgibbon, 'Together on the Way', *The Furrow*, 68, October 2017; and Gerry O'Hanlon, 'The Joy of Love – *Amoris Laetitia*, *The Furrow*, 67, June 2016, 328–36, at 335–36.
285 See Chapter Eight of this book in particular.
286 See Gerry O'Hanlon, 'Vatican II as a Resource for the Renewal of the Church in Ireland in the Twenty-First Century', in Dermot A. Lane (ed.), *Vatican II in Ireland, Fifty Years On*, op. cit., 219–36, at 227–30.

family.[287] They noted that '… many of those who responded to the questionnaire expressed particular difficulties with the teaching on extra-marital sex and cohabitation by unmarried couples, divorce and remarriage, family planning, assisted reproduction, homosexuality. The Church's teaching in these sensitive areas is often not experienced as realistic, compassionate or life-enhancing. Some see it as disconnected from real-life experience, leaving them feeling guilty and excluded. We recognise our responsibility as bishops to present faithfully the Church's teaching on marriage and the family in a positive and engaging way, whilst showing compassion and mercy towards those who are finding difficulty in accepting or living it'.

This statement is interesting because it indicates a welcome realism and compassion towards those who find Church teaching in these areas difficult. But does it also show an unnecessarily restricted understanding of their own role as bishops with regard to this teaching? Might not a more vigorous embrace of collegiality allow for the possibility that the bishops might take seriously the difficulty the faithful have in receiving the teaching, having regard to their own responsibility as bishops to be in touch with 'the sense of faith' of their own faithful, and might they not use this as a resource in the authentic expression of their teaching office?

It can seem that too often – in the Irish Church but more universally as well – there has developed a kind of habit of interpreting the injunction on bishops to 'teach faithfully' as being simply identical with teaching what Rome says, without sufficient regard to listening carefully to what people in good faith experience in their lives, and without sufficient regard also to the authoritative status of the teaching in question. A more collegial approach would take more account of 'the sense of the faithful', while being careful to test and discern this in the light of Scripture, Tradition, theological opinion and maintaining communion with other local Churches and the

---

287 Statement of the Irish Catholic Bishops' Conference regarding the questionnaire from the Synod on the Family, Thursday 13 March 2014.

universal Church.[288] It is striking, as noted, that on an issue like family and sexuality, that involves such an obvious disconnect in our part of the world between Church doctrine and the experience and practice of the faithful, that the bishops would focus on better communication of a message that in some parts the faithful simply do not accept. But this response, in the longer term, is limited because it does not address the underlying unease of the faithful with respect to the content of the teaching itself.

This is what was adverted to by Bishop Johan Bonny in his pre-synodal contribution when he argued that in many issues to do with sexuality and gender the '... antithesis between "pastoral care" and "doctrine" is inappropriate in both theological and pastoral terms and it has no foundation in the tradition of the Church.'[289] Bonny goes on to call for a reconsideration of both pastoral care and doctrine. It should be recalled again in this context that Pope Francis urges bishops to listen to the faithful and not simply to those who would tell them what they would like to hear (EG, 31).

One thinks also, in this context, of the almost fatalistic acceptance of the clunky English translation of the Missal which continues to be a burdensome obstacle to liturgical worship for so many. Can we discover that 'better balance of vital forces' which Orsy speaks about and which a synodal Church aims to address, in matters such as the autonomy of local bishops and their duty to act together in conference, as well as the duty of bishops to teach with authority, but to do so by regarding the 'sense of the faithful' as a constitutive element in 'thinking with the church'? The late Sean Freyne, writing in 1993, saw the Irish Episcopal Conference 'as having a serious image problem, perceived more as a collective of Vatican civil servants than as pastors with a genuinely independent concern for the real needs of their flocks'.[290] A more collegial approach requires a

288 See Richard R. Gaillardetz, *When the Magisterium Intervenes*, Collegeville, MN: Liturgical Press, 2012, and, in particular, the article by Ormond Rush, 'The Prophetic Office in the Church: Pneumatological Perspective on the *Sensus Fidelium* – Theology-Magisterium Relationship', 89–112. See also Gaillardetz, *By What Authority?* Collegeville, MN: Liturgical Press, 2003.
289 Bishop Johan Bonny, 'The Synod on the Family – a Bishop's expectations', *The Furrow*, 65, October 2014, 455–56 (455–64 – an abridged version of Bonny's original text).
290 Sean Freyne, 'What Crisis? Some Thoughts on Irish Catholicism', *The Furrow*, 44/10, October 1993, 538.

change not just in theological understanding but also in imagination: bishops, theologically, are not simply papal delegates, they have an independent authority, but they need too to begin to imagine how to exercise this independence in a way that is respectful of the need for unity, for communion. The unity in question needs to respect diversity more than hitherto – this is what Cardinal Lehmann of Mainz seemed to be suggesting when he was reported as saying: 'We need to be more courageous in dialogue within the Church. We complain that Rome is over-powerful but that is because we are too weak'.[291] And this seems also to be the direction in which Pope Francis himself is pointing when he speaks again and again of the need for a more collegial, less centralised Church, in which consultation must be real and not just token, in which 'thinking with the Church' involves not just obeying the Magisterium but listening to the 'sense of faith' of the People of God.[292] There are many new voices within the Irish Episcopal Conference: might there not be an opportunity then for an audit of the conference's mode of proceeding and a hope that this could develop into a real instrument of leadership more responsive to today's situation?

Bishops (as Cardinal Cupich[293] noted) can be tempted to view this approach as too onerous, involving many organisational problems, and prefer to 'go solo'. It can seem easier to 'get things done' by simple fiat as opposed to seemingly interminable group meetings and discussion. And laity may share the sense of some of the disparaging remarks of some bishops about the proliferation of mere 'talking shops', without real consequences. But, as we noted, this is not a recipe for success in a culture which values inclusion and participation, and, besides, is not faithful to the Church's own theology of the role of the baptised. The recent Synod on the Family, in a modest but real way, illustrated how thorny matters can be discussed, often with considerable conflict and disagreement, and still with a discerning love which resulted in concrete results for the situation of the divorced and remarried in particular. Similarly many

291 *The Tablet*, 15 March 2014, 33.
292 Interview with Jesuit journals, 2013; *Evangelii Gaudium*, 2013, 102, 119, 126, 198.
293 See Joshua J. McElwee, 'Cardinal Cupich: Francis is giving new life to Vatican II reforms', *National Catholic Reporter*, 13 March 2017.

women – and men – will have been encouraged by the establishment of a commission to study the issue of female deacons, in response to considerable representation on the issue. The Synod of Limerick fits into this evolving framework: it enabled a deeper renewal and conversion within the diocese, part of which was due to the skilled and prayerful way in which open debate was allowed to flourish.

Francis's maxim that 'time is greater than space' (EG, 222 ff) encourages us to engage in processes that are more likely to lead to long-term change that is durable rather than short-term quick results that are often the result of power plays. This seems absolutely the right approach for the Irish Catholic Church, faced as it is by the crisis that has been described here. A few years ago the recently retired Bishop of Ossory, Seamus Freeman, promised the beginnings of a 'structured dialogue' at national level within the Irish Church, in response to Pope Benedict's Letter to Irish Catholics (*The Irish Times,* 28 December 2010). The Association of Catholic Priests, in a meeting with representatives of the Irish Episcopal Conference (May 2016), offered to help organise a national synod of the Irish Church, and has continued to make this offer.

It would be wonderful if the bishops could offer such leadership in the future, perhaps spurred on by the World Meeting of Families (WMF) event and papal visit. The Irish Episcopal Conference has shown its ability to organise major events (think of the Eucharistic Congress in 2012 and now, with the lead role being taken by the Archdiocese of Dublin, the WMF in 2018). One senses that both these major events, while involving a great deal of consultation and sharing, were still very much governed by a top-down, content-focused, catechetical methodology, with consultation focused on prepared texts. Could the bishops – as the Pope is suggesting – risk a more open, process-centred approach, in which the first step would be a listening to the real desires, hopes, fears, doubts and joys of the faithful – and then move to engage all this with Church teaching in a reciprocal movement which would involve ongoing change?

Bishops might understandably fear a certain loss of control in such a scenario and may fear that they cannot deliver on raised expectations. But we have enough experience in individual dioceses by now to know that this is not a real reason for not trying – people welcome open debate warmly, as long as they believe they are being taken seriously. They do not expect instant solutions, or that the Irish bishops on their own can change everything. They are just glad to be empowered to speak and listen, and appreciate when decisions follow at local level or when their conclusions on more contested issues of significance to the whole Church are fed openly into the universal Church in an ongoing process of assessment and discernment.

Bishops might say, well, what if we do have a national synod, what then? Well, apart from the renewal and reform generated by the preparation and the synod itself, we then have – another national synod! This is, as Francis makes clear, a permanent way of being Church, not some kind of occasional novelty. Bishops might also say we don't have the necessary infrastructure yet, in some parishes there aren't even parish councils – but, besides the fact that much of this infrastructure is already in place, notice that we were going to have a synod would serve to rally the dilatory, galvanise the energy of the committed and, conceivably, mobilise the interest of young people and the disaffected as well.

Post-Catholic Ireland need not fall prey to the dominant trend of de-institutionalisation and individualisation, with an extra-institutional religion that is practised with vitality only outside the institutional Catholic Church, and an institutional remnant that is culturally irrelevant. However, without a serious commitment to reform and renewal that seems the likely future. Pope Francis is giving a pointer to a different model of Church, based on deeper conversion to Jesus Christ, missionary in its approach to the great issues facing humanity and our world, respectful of both personal conscience and Magisterium, and entailing a synodal form of Church at all levels. This must surely be the way forward for the Irish Church, as many have long argued. It would be wonderful if the bishops could give this type of leadership.

Archbishop Eamon Martin, participant with Archbishop

Diarmuid Martin[294] at the Synod on the Family, is reported to have said he came back to Ireland a 'changed' man after the synod, obviously appreciative of the experience. In particular he noted the imperative to 'go out, to listen and to integrate more into the life of the Church those who may be hitherto on the peripheries'.[295] It would be wonderful if the transformative experience enjoyed by Irish bishops at the Synod in Rome were replicated throughout the Church in Ireland itself. This should not be disparaged as more 'talking shops', as if the process of inclusive talking and listening were somehow a distraction, a poor second to proclamation of the Word. What is a synod, a synodal Church, but 'a talking shop', one where all together journey, listening, talking and then acting, an acting that will include a richer proclamation of the Word on the basis of the listening and speaking that have gone before? And is this not what Pope Francis has asked the Church to embark on? Is it not the desire of Francis that the faithful at local level share the inspiring experience of Irish bishops at the universal level?

It would be a mistake to suppose that simply bringing back the 'good news' from this synod at Rome or any similar exercise will be enough. All the People of God, like our two archbishops, need to be part of the conversation – remember, in 2010 retired Bishop Seamus Freeman promised us a 'structured dialogue' within the Irish Church.

What is required now is an acceleration and intensification of this process in Ireland.[296] Our two archbishops, after their recent experience, are in an ideal position to give the lead here. It would be so sad, and ironic, if so much energy – and finance – were put into the preparation of a future papal visit, seen as a kind of a *deus*

---

294 I note the reported words of Archbishop Diarmuid Martin, referring back to a meeting with Pope Francis in September 2015, that the World Meeting of Families '... is not an isolated event ... it belongs with a process of discernment and encouragement, of accompaniment and animation of families ... it belongs within a programme of renewal ... it will be an important milestone in the application of the synodal process and of the apostolic exhortation', *The Irish Times*, 25 May 2016.

295 *The Irish Catholic*, 29 October 2015.

296 For more on this and the kind of spirituality of change that would facilitate it, see Gerry O'Hanlon, 'The People of God: Towards a Renewed Church?', in Suzanne Mulligan (ed.), *Reaping the Harvest: Fifty Years after Vatican II*, Dublin: Columba Press, 2012, 63–87, at 79–87.

ex machina response to our challenges, when the pope himself is calling for a less centralised, more collegial and synodal Church. Let us use this visit, if it is to happen, as a catalyst towards a more synodal Irish Church, by announcing the convocation of a series of national assemblies of the Irish Church, and so letting everyone – including the Pope – know that we are serious about implementing his vision.

Co-leadership by others

It will help bishops to give this kind of leadership if all the faithful, including priests and religious, make it clear that this is what they want and exercise their own calling to leadership accordingly.[297] Can the lay faithful, priests and religious resist the temptation to inertia or passive resistance and find a way to get involved, at whatever level, in promoting a more inclusive Church, and signal our willingness to help our bishops in their complex and daunting task?

There is a particular challenge to priests here. As they age, and are tempted to fall back on the kind of rationalisation which justifies a 'business as usual' attitude that 'will see me out', can they be helped to resist and to be responsive to the needs of their communities? So many priests are dearly loved by their local communities, despite the reputational damage to the priesthood in general due to the terrible abuse scandal. Can they be helped to draw energy from this well-deserved local appreciation and respect, an energy directed towards a more participative Church, with a particular reach-out to young adults?

Can reform groups in particular continue to be true to their own charism and mission, but also consider the wisdom of Sidney Tarrow when he stressed the particular significance of 'political opportunity' (in this case the election of Francis as a reforming pope) in the struggle for any justice cause, and the wisdom of arguing for access to input and power when such an opportunity presents itself, rather than opting for singular and concrete gains which have less lasting significance?[298]

---

297 See Gerry O'Hanlon, 'Ireland and the Quiet Revolution in the Catholic Church', *The Furrow*, 68, May 2017, 259–67, at 267.
298 Sidney G. Tarrow, *Power in Movement, Social Movements and Contentious Politics*,

It is easy to miss the wood for the trees in these matters. There is a quiet revolution going on in the Catholic Church, with enormous significance for now but even more for future generations, including in Ireland. It will not be accomplished overnight. But is has a better chance of success if we recognise what is at its core – the structural and cultural transformation of the Church along synodal, collegial lines in order to give better witness to the Good News of Jesus Christ for our times – and we in Ireland have our role to play here.

Conclusion

I have made the case that we in Ireland can be helped enormously to address the crisis in the Catholic Church by a determined, planned and sustained adoption of Pope Francis's strategic and visionary project of a synodal transformation of the Catholic Church at all levels, always in the context of a faith encounter with Jesus Christ and a commitment to his mission. For this to occur, good leadership at local level is required – by bishops, first of all, but also by laity, priests and religious. We have a right to demand no less of one another.

There would be enormous value in placing our current crisis in the context of a synodal Church, with capacity to conduct open and honest debate internally and with society in general, and to mobilise all our resources in planning together for the future.[299] It would also encourage the Church to adopt a less anxious, paternalistic mode of moral guardianship within the Church and towards society at large, and move to a more Socratic, midwifery mode of teaching as persuasion, in which more trust is placed in adult laity to internalise values, rather than accept applied teaching on grounds of authority alone. This might mean that, along the lines of the Courtyard of the Gentiles project initiated by Pope Benedict and promoted by the Pontifical Council for Culture, the Catholic Church in Ireland would consider the more active promotion of conferences and public dialogues in which prominent public intellectuals of all faiths

Cambridge: Cambridge University Press, 2011, 159–67 – see O'Hanlon, 'Voices of Hope: Echoes of the Divine', *Doctrine and Life*, 64, January 2014, 38–52, at 48–52.

299 See Gerry O'Hanlon, 'A Challenge to the Churches', in G. O'Hanlon (ed.), *A Dialogue of Hope*, Dublin: Messenger Publications, 2017, 108–22, at 112–13.

and none would engage in conversations about human flourishing in Ireland. The voices of the artistic community – poets, novelists, dramatists and others – would be invaluable in this context. In this and in other ways (building 'bridges of new and perhaps surprising partnerships') the Church can be part of a national dialogue which takes religion seriously, sometimes as initiator and sometimes as participant at the invitation of others. Interestingly the website for this Vatican project asks is it not the case that the real divide today is '… no longer between those who believe and do not believe in God … but between those who recognise the gift of culture and history, of grace and gratuity, and those who found everything on the cult of efficiency, be it sacral or science?'[300] With such a culture and practice of deeper debate in place, the Church would be in a better position to engage with greater credibility in public issues of dispute like same-sex marriage and the constitutional ban on abortion.

The Church would also be illustrating in public practice that far from being a fear- and rule-based religion, buttressed by a kind of blind and unquestioning conformity to formal authority, Catholicism is essentially (and can be in reality) a liberating reality, that, to use perhaps surprising terms, the gospels are (before their time) truly documents of radical Enlightenment and Liberation, showing a way to the kind of love that is not illusory, self-created or oblivious of human suffering and evil – the joy of the gospel.

However, what also emerges is that for this reality to be seen as liberating requires ongoing and open dialogue and conversation internally and with our culture, in order to be sensitive to where the Good News of God's merciful love in Jesus Christ can resonate with human need and desire. This, again, will not happen overnight: the embedding of such a culture will require time, perhaps generations, to achieve. But what can start and happen overnight is the explicit first steps towards this kind of goal: the public adoption of the revolutionary synodal project of Church by Catholicism in Ireland would open all kinds of gates to the future and give the faithful a sense of purpose, energy and hope. The best way of taking

---

300 See www.cultura.va/content/cultura/en/dipartimenti/ateismo-e-non-credenza/perche-il-cortile-di-gentile -html

this first step, building on what is already in place, would be the convocation of a first national assembly of the Catholic Church in Ireland, drawing on the assistance and experience of other Christian Churches, and with invited participants from those of other and no faiths.[301]

301 See Gerry O'Hanlon, 'Towards a National Consultation of the Faithful', *The Furrow*, 62, February 2011, 88–93.

CONCLUSION

And nobody puts new wine into old wineskins; if he does, the wine
will burst the skins, and the wine is lost and the skins too. No! New
wine, fresh skins. (Mk 2:22)

The Jesus of the gospels is always respectful of tradition and the old
(Moses, the Law, John the Baptist), and yet confidently proclaiming
the new, 'But I say to you ... I will send the Holy Spirit who will
lead you into the fullness of truth' (Jn 16:7-13). Yes, salvation is
surely for the Jewish people, but, gradually, and after much conflict
and struggle, it became clear that it was also for the Gentiles. This
respect for tradition and yet awareness that with Jesus something
radically new had been introduced, was something that did not
end with New Testament times. Rather, it was understood by the
Church to be constitutive of its being, as it undertook to embed its
mission in constantly changing cultures. And so, the need to address
the idiom of Greco-Roman metaphysics in the doctrinal debates
of the early centuries, the influence of medieval feudalism on the
structures and doctrines of the scholastic era, the post-Reformation
and Enlightenment conversation which is still ongoing. All through
these times the model of Church itself changed, according to the
needs of particular ages and cultures.

Now, in a post-modern culture, this reciprocal conversation
between Church and culture continues. As Michael Conway notes,
we live at a time when the old hegemony of Church and state is
being replaced by multiple other actors – conventional and social
media, civil society, advocacy groups and, above all, the centrality
of the autonomous and free individual.[302] People are more interested
in this life than the next, in authenticity rather than conformity, in
the narrative and experiential rather than the metaphysical, in what
is to be freely appropriated as meaningful rather than on what is

302 Michael A. Conway, 'Changing Foundations: Identity, Church and Culture', *The Furrow, 69,*
    February 2018, 90–103.

imposed by lawful authority. All this requires ecclesial institutional change too.

We cannot, dare not, simply ignore this contemporary culture and focus solely on pointing out its shortcomings. To do so is to adopt a tone deaf approach incapable of touching people with the Good News, an approach with an exclusive, and hence reductive, focus on the weak points of modernity and post-modernity. In the end metaphysics too is important, authority and the common good are needed as much as individual freedom, analysis, as well as a narrative of experience, is required, we need to reflect on the next life as well as this one – but this counter-balancing will only happen, paradoxically, if we are fully, yet critically, immersed in our own culture, learning from as well as teaching the world as the Second Vatican Council understood.

Pope Francis has proposed a synodal model of Church, rooted in a faith encounter with Jesus Christ and committed to his mission, as the appropriate institutional response to our changed world and faithful to Christian tradition. After the 'lamentations' of more recent times, he has directed the Church in an unambiguous way back to the ecclesiology of the Second Vatican Council, with its focus on collegiality and conciliarity. This has the merit of retrieving ancient Christian truths (like collegiality itself and the sense of the faithful), as well as offering a more inclusive, participative and conversational space in which individuals and communities can negotiate their own identities with integrity today. This 'inverted pyramid' model of Church, a revolutionary paradigm shift which values decentralisation and subsidiarity, consultation and open debate, and dialogue internally and with our culture is more attuned to the spirit of the age while retaining, through its notion of 'communal discernment', the ability to distinguish critically between mere fad and whispers of the Spirit that are authentic.

A Church that is 'entirely synodal' at all levels will respect the fundamental equality of all the baptised and be critical of clericalism; it will offer spaces for the sharing of faith, doubts and searchings for truth among its members, with outreach to the alienated and fellow searchers at a time of deepening secularisation; it will be conscious of the mission to announce and facilitate the coming of the Kingdom of God by its socio-economic, environmental critique and its privileging of the lens of the poor; it will respect the disquiet among the faithful caused by certain neuralgic teachings and be a catalyst for a sound doctrinal development; it will offer the promise of more accountable governance, with the involvement of laity, including, of course, women. It will, in short, be a 'field-hospital' to those who suffer and are troubled, and a more attractive icon to everyone of the Jesus Christ who captivated his disciples with his authority, mercy and tenderness, and his intimacy with the one he called Abba. It will dare to propose nothing less than a call to holiness for all the baptised.[303]

Francis himself knows that a change of attitude and culture is even more important than one of structure and institution. This will require time, even if a start can be made immediately. But he also recognises that change of structure, institution and even law go hand-in-hand with that of attitude, and the two are mutually reinforcing. One of the less noted but essential elements contributing to the success of the Good Friday/Belfast agreement was its comprehensive codification in law and its implementation through agreed structures and institutions. And so there will be many different ways of embedding synodality in Church practice – including through adult formation, prayer and liturgy, parish councils and ecumenical learning – but these must also include changes in structures, institutions and law, including, from time to time, formal synods or assemblies at all levels of Church life. These must be seen not simply as exceptional events involving extraordinary preparation but must become part of the regular rhythm of Church life.[304]

I have noted several times that this call to a new way of being Church does not depend on the pope himself being always right on every matter. Francis has been the first to confess that he is a

303 See in particular *Gaudete et Exsultate,* the Apostolic Exhortation of Pope Francis, April 2018, described as his 'spiritual masterpiece' (*The Tablet,* 14 April 2018, 2).
304 This approach is confirmed by the release on May 3, 2018 of a document by the International Theological Commission, under the Presidency of Bishop Ladaria and approved for publication by Pope Francis on March 2, 2018, called Synodality in the Life and Mission of the Church, see Joshua J. McAlwee, Consult the laity, Vatican theological commission says, May 4 2018, www.ncronline.org/news/vatican/consult-laity-theological-commission-says

sinner, and has apologised since taking up his role as pope for times when he got things wrong. We all have feet of clay, we contain the treasure of the Good News in 'èarthen vessels' (2 Co 4:7). I have argued, however, that in this instance he has made a crucially correct diagnosis and prognosis of ecclesial ills and remedies. And, of course, central to this diagnosis, is his call to reform the papacy itself, to allow it to function less in splendid isolation and more in tune with its mission to be a focus of unity and love (including with other Churches) and to 'strengthen the others' (including the role of all the lay faithful) (Lk 22:32).

I have noted the opposition to the project proposed by Francis. In a curious way that opposition which is most open and even vehement is also that which is most understandable and manageable: as he himself has noted, it is normal that strong views are held and expressed, and if synodality and the communal discernment which is at its core are to flourish then they must be capable of handling such opposition (as was true of the early Church). More worrying, ironically, is the kind of lack of understanding, apathy and even passive aggression, which effectively ignores what Francis is saying, or, more charitably, puts it on the back burner, perhaps not yet seeing its crucial visionary and strategic importance.

It is the latter response which seems to be more characteristic of the Irish Catholic Church and the Irish media, and I have been making the argument that all the faithful, and in particular our leaders, are being invited urgently to respond in a more focused and energetic way to what Francis is saying. A clear indicator that this was happening would be an announcement by the Irish Episcopal Conference that a synodal Church is the Church of the future, and, in that context, the convocation of a national assembly or synod in the near future, as the first in a series of regular assemblies. This is the kind of bold signal which would give people hope, would galvanise their participation, and would be an opportunity to engage with young people in particular, many of whom are indifferent now to an institution that accords them no voice. The Catholic Church in Ireland, in response to the promptings of the Spirit articulated through the call of Francis, can seize this opportunity to walk along the road together with the Stranger, in sure hope of recognising him as the Lord in the breaking of bread – that joyful experience of the disciples on the road to Emmaus, who said afterwards 'did not our hearts burn within us?' (Lk 24:32).

SELECT BIBLIOGRAPHY

Books

Campbell, Anthony F., *The Whisper of Spirit, A Believable God Today*, Grand Rapids, MI/ Cambridge, UK: William Eeerdmans, 2008.

Ciorra, Anthony and Higgins, Michael D. (eds), *Vatican II, A Universal Call to Holiness*, New York, NY/Mahwah, NJ: Paulist Press, 2012.

Claffey, Patrick, Egan, Joe, and Keenan, Marie (eds), *Broken Faith, Why Hope Matters*, Bern: Peter Lang, 2013.

Coll, Niall (ed.), *Ireland and Vatican II*, Dublin: Columba Press, 2015.

Corkery, James and Worcester, Thomas (eds), *The Papacy since 1500*, Cambridge: Cambridge University Press, 2010.

Daly, Gabriel, *The Church, Always in Need of Reform*, Dublin: Dominican Publications, 2015.

Dulles, Avery, *Models of the Church*, Dublin: Gill & Macmillan, second edition, 1988.

Faggioli, Massimo, *Vatican II, The Battle for Meaning*, Mahwah, NJ: Paulist Press, 2012.

___ *Pope Francis, Tradition in Transition*, New York, NY/Mahwah, NJ: Paulist Press, 2015.

___*Catholicism and Citizenship, Political Cultures of the Church in the Twenty-First Century*, Collegeville, MN: Liturgical Press, 2017.

Flannery, Tony, *A Question of Conscience*, Dublin: Londubh Books, 2013.

Gaillardetz, Richard R., *By What Authority? A Primer on Scripture, the Magisterium, and the Sense of the Faithful*, Collegeville, MN: Liturgical Press, 2003.

___ (ed.), *When the Magisterium Intervenes*, Collegeville, MN: Liturgical Press, 2012.

Gaillardetz, Richard R., and Catherine E. Clifford (eds), *Keys to the Council, Unlocking the Teaching of Vatican II*, Collegeville, MN: Liturgical Press, 2012.

Gaillardetz, Richard R., *An Unfinished Council, Vatican II, Pope Francis, and the Renewal of Catholicism*, Collegeville, MN: Liturgical Press, 2015.

Gaillardetz, Richard R., and Hahnenberg, Edward P., *A Church with Open Doors, Catholic Ecclesiology for the Third Millennium*, Collegeville, MN: Liturgical Press, 2015.

Gallagher, Michael Paul, *Clashing Symbols, An Introduction to Faith and Culture*, London: Darton, Longman & Todd, 1997.

Ganiel, Gladys, *Transforming Post-Catholic Ireland, Religious Practice in Post-Modernity*, Oxford: Oxford University Press, 2016.

Heiding, Frederik, *Ignatian Spirituality at Ecclesial Frontiers*, Oxford: Oxford University Press, 2012.

Hinze, Bradford E., *Prophetic Obedience, Ecclesiology for a Dialogical Church*, New York, NY: Orbis, 2016.

Hoban, Brendan, *Where do we go from here? The Crisis in Irish Catholicism*, Mayo: Banley House, 2012.

___ *Who will break the bread for us? Disappearing Priests*, Mayo: Banley House, 2013.

International Theological Commission, *'Sensus Fidei' in the Life of the Church*, 10 June 2014.

___ *Synodality in the Life and Mission of the Church*, 2 March 2018.

Ivereigh, Austin, *The Great Reformer, Francis and the making of a radical Pope*, London: Allen & Unwin, 2014.

Lacy, Michael J., and Oakley, Francis (eds), *The Crisis of Authority in Catholic Modernity*, Oxford: Oxford University Press, 2011.

Lane, Dermot A. (ed.), *Vatican II in Ireland, Fifty Years On*, Bern: Peter Lang, 2015.

Lane, Dermot A., *Catholic Education in the Light of Vatican II and Laudato Si'*, Dublin: Veritas, 2015.

Lash, Nicholas, *Theology for Pilgrims*, London: Darton, Longman & Todd, 2008.

Lonergan, Bernard J. F., *Insight, A Study of Human Understanding*, London: Longmans, Green & Co, 1957.

Maher, Eamon and O'Brien, Eugene (eds), *Tracing the Cultural Legacy of Irish Catholicism*, Manchester: Manchester University Press, 2017.

McAleese, Mary, *Quo Vadis, Collegiality in the Code of Canon Law*, Dublin: Columba Press, 2012.

McBrien, Richard P., *The Church, The Evolution of Catholicism*, New York, NY: HarperOne, 2009.

McDonagh, Enda (ed.), *Performing the Word, Festschrift for Ronan Drury,* Dublin: Columba Press, 2014.

Mulligan, Suzanne (ed.), *Reaping the Harvest: Fifty Years after Vatican II,* Dublin: Columba Press, 2012.

O'Donnell, Christopher, *Ecclesia, A Theological Encylopedia of the Church,* Collegeville, MN: Liturgical Press, 1996.

O'Malley, John W., *What Happened at Vatican II,* Harvard, MA: Harvard University Press, 2008.

Orsy, Ladislas, *Probing the Spirit, A Theological Evaluation of Communal Discernment,* New Jersey: Dimension Books, 1976.

___ *Receiving the Council,* Collegeville, MN: Liturgical Press, 2009.

Politi, Marco, *Pope Francis Among the Wolves,* New York: Columbia University Press, 2015.

Puglisi, James F. (ed.), *How Can the Petrine Ministry Be a Service to the Unity of the Universal Church?,* Grand Rapids, MI/Cambridge, UK: William B. Eeerdmans, 2010.

Rahner, Karl, *Free Speech in the Church,* New York, NY: Sheed and Ward, 1959.

Ratzinger, Joseph, *Principles for Catholic Theology: Building Stones for a Fundamental Theology,* San Francisco, CA: Ignatius Press, 1987.

Rausch, Thomas P. and Gaillardetz, Richard R. (eds.), *Go Into the Streets! The Welcoming Church of Pope Francis,* New Jersey: Paulist Press, 2016.

Sullivan, Francis A., *Magisterium: Teaching Authority in the Catholic Church,* Dublin: Gill & Macmillan, 1983.

Sullivan, Francis A., *Creative Fidelity, Weighing and Interpreting Documents of the Magisterium,* Dublin: Gill & Macmillan, 1996.

Tarrow, Sidney G., *Power in Movement, Social Movements and Contentious Politics,* Cambridge: Cambridge University Press, 2011.

Toner, Jules, *Discerning God's Will,* St Louis, MO: Institute of Jesuit Sources, 1991.

Vallely, Paul, *Pope Francis, Untying the Knots,* London: Bloomsbury, 2013.

Articles

Bacq, Philip, 'La relation home-femme dans la société occidentale et la tradition de l'Église', *En Question,* 110, septembre 2014, 27–9, and 'Tradition chrétienne et évolution de la Famille', *Études,* mars 2014, 29–39.

Berten, Ignace, 'Le synode sur la famille. Quels enjeux pour l'Église et pour les communautés chrétiennes?', *En Question,* 112, mars 2015, 19–22.

Bonny, Bishop Johan, 'Synod on the Family, Expectations of a Diocesan Bishop, Antwerp, September 1, 2014', *The Furrow,* 65, October 2014.

Callaghan, Brendan, 'On Scandals and scandals: the psychology of clerical paedophilia', *Studies,* 99, autumn 2010, 343–56.

Carroll, Denis, 'A Note on Dissent, Theological and Otherwise', *Studies,* spring 1987, 29–41.

Conway, Michael A., 'Ministry in Transition', *The Furrow,* 65, March 2014, 131–49.

___ 'Christianity in Europe – a Future?' *The Furrow,* 65, July–August, 2014, 331–8.

___ 'New Beginnings and Painful Endings', *The Furrow,* 68, May 2017, 268–78.

___ 'Faith-life, Church and Institution', *The Furrow,* 68, September 2017, 461–74.

___ 'Changing Foundations: Identity, Church and Culture', *The Furrow,* 69, February 2018, 90–103.

Corkery, Jim, 'The Catholic Church in Ireland: "What must we do?" (Acts 2:37)', *Studies,* 100, summer 2011, 193–205.

___ 'Whither Catholicism in Ireland?', *Studies,* 101, winter 2012, 387–96.

___ 'Our Own Hope Had Been … ' (Luke 24: 21)': *The Promise of Vatican II – Reality or Illusion?,* in Suzanne Mulligan (ed.), *Reaping the Harvest: Fifty Years after Vatican II,* Dublin: Columba Press, 2012, 13–37.

___ 'Speak Freely – but watch your back! Dissent and Dissenters in the Catholic Church Today', *Doctrine and Life,* 62, December 2012, 10–22.

___ 'The Reception of Vatican II in Ireland', in Dermot A. Lane (ed.), *Vatican II in Ireland, Fifty Years On,* Bern: Peter Lang, 2015, 97–119.

De Gaulmyn, Isabelle, 'Will Pope Francis' Reforms Last?', *La Croix,* 1 June 2017.

Duffy, Eugene, 'Assembly or Synod?', *The Furrow,* 63, June 2012, 295–303.

___ 'Reimaging the Church in Ireland in the Light of Vatican II', in Niall Coll (ed.), *Ireland and Vatican II*, Dublin: Columba Press, 2015, 113–29.

Fitzgibbon, Eamonn, 'Together on the Way – Pope Francis and Synodality', *The Furrow*, 68, October 2017, 532–9.

Freyne, Sean, 'What Crisis? Some Thoughts on Irish Catholicism', *The Furrow*, 44, October 1993.

Fuller, Louise, 'Revisiting the faith of our fathers … and reimagining its relevance in the context of twenty-first century Ireland', in Eamon Maher and Eugene O'Brien (eds), *Tracing the Cultural Legacy of Irish Catholicism*, Manchester: Manchester University Press, 2017, 38–52.

Gaillardetz, Richard R., 'The Pastoral Orientation of Doctrine', in Rausch and Gaillardetz (eds), *Go Into the Streets!*, Mahwah, NJ: Paulist Press, 2016, 125–40.

Gaillardetz, Richard, 'Is the Pope a Catholic?', *The Tablet*, 7 October 2017, 4–5.

___ 'Power and Authority in the Church: Emerging Issues', in Richard R. Gaillardetz and Edward P. Hahnenberg (eds), *A Church with Open Doors*, Collegeville, MN: Liturgical Press, 2015, 87–111.

Gallagher, Gerard, 'Millennial Matters – Reconnecting the Disconnected', *The Furrow*, 68, September 2017, 479–87.

Gallagher, Raphael, 'The Synod – A Fresh Pastoral Journey', *The Furrow*, 67, September 2015, 439–46.

Ganiel, Gladys, 'Ireland as a Post-Catholic Religious Market? The Role of Extra-Institutional Religion', *Studies*, 106, spring 2017, 31–8.

Hahnenberg, Edward P., Learning from Experience: Attention to Anomalies in a Theology of Ministry, in Richard R. Gaillardetz and Edward P. Hahnenberg (eds), *A Church with Open Doors*, Collegeville, MN: Liturgical Press, 2015, 159–80.

Hannon, Patrick, 'Free Speech in the Church?', *The Furrow*, 63, June 2012, 259–68.

___ 'Church and State in Ireland; Perspectives of Vatican II', in Dermot A. Lane (ed.), *Vatican II in Ireland: Fifty Years On*, Bern: Peter Lang, 2015, 359–82.

Harold-Barry, David, 'A Toledo Dungeon – Is the Irish Church in a "Dark Night"?', *The Furrow*, 68, December 2017, 668–72.

Hinsdale, Mary-Ann, 'A Feminist Reflection on Post-Conciliar Catholic Ecclesiology', in Richard R. Gaillardetz and Edward P. Hahnenberg (eds), *A Church with Open Doors*, Collegeville, MN: Liturgical Press, 112–37.

Hinze, Bradford E., 'Listening to the Spirit', *The Tablet*, 3 June 2017, 4–5.

___ 'A Decade of Disciplining Theologians', in Richard R. Gaillardetz (ed.), *When the Magisterium Intervenes*, Collgeville, MN: Liturgical Press, 2012, 3–39.

Honohan, Iseult, 'Religious Perspective in the Public Sphere', in Gerry O'Hanlon (ed.), *A Dialogue of Hope*, Dublin: Messenger Publications, 2017, 36–48.

Inglis, Tom, 'Church and Culture in Catholic Ireland', *Studies*, 106, spring 2017, 21–30.

Komonchak, Joseph A., 'Benedict XVI and the Interpretation of Vatican II', in Michael J. Lacy and Francis Oakley (eds), *The Crisis of Authority in Catholic Modernity*, Oxford: Oxford University Press, 93–110.

Lacy, Michael, 'The Problem of Authority and its Limits', in Michael J. Lacy and Francis Oakley (eds), *The Crisis of Authority in Catholic Modernity*, Oxford: Oxford University Press, 2011, 1–25.

Lane, Dermot A., 'A Pastor looks Back and Forward', *The Furrow*, 68, October 2017, 547–53.

Mallon, Colleen Mary, 'Gracious Resistance, Religious Women Charting an Ecclesial Path', in Richard R. Gaillardetz (ed.), *When the Magisterium Intervenes*, Collegeville, MN: Liturgical Press, 2012, 63–85.

Mannion, Gerard, 'Re-Engaging the People of God', Thomas P. Rausch and Richard R. Gaillardetz (eds), *Go Into The Streets!*, Mahwah, NJ: Paulist Press, 2016, 57–75.

___ 'A Teaching Church That Learns? Discerning "Authentic" Teaching in our Times', in Michael J. Lacy and Francis Oakley (eds), *The Crisis of Authority in Catholic Modernity*, Oxford: Oxford University Press, 2011, 161–91.

Martin, Archbishop Diarmuid, 'A Post-Catholic Ireland? Renewing the Irish Church from Within', *America*, 20 May 2013.

___ '"Keeping the Show on the Road": Is This the Future of the Irish Catholic Church?', Address to the Cambridge Group for Irish Studies at Magdalene College, Cambridge, 22 February 2011.

McElwee, Joshua J., 'Pope Francis has endeavoured to shift church culture', *National Catholic Reporter*, June 2016, 328–36.

___ Cardinal Cupich: 'Francis is giving new life to Vatican II reforms', *National Catholic Reporter*, 13 March 2017.

Orsy, Ladislas, 'Where is Our Church Going? searching for a response', *The Furrow*, 63, December 2012, 591–5.

___ 'Fifty Years later: the Council lives', *Doctrine and Life*, 62, October 2012, 5–11.

Rahner, Karl, 'Structural Change in the Church of the Future', *Theological Investigations*, vol. 20, London: Darton, Longman & Todd, 1981, 115–32.

Reese, Thomas, 'Reforming the Vatican, What the Church Can Learn from Other Institutions', *Commonweal*, 25 April 2008.

___ 'How Pope Francis can reform the Vatican Curia', *National Catholic Reporter*, 25 March 2013.

Riordan, Patrick, 'A Blessed Rage for the Common Good', *Irish Theological Quarterly*, 76, 2011, 3–19.

Ruddy, Christopher, 'The Local and Universal Church', in Rausch and Gaillardetz (eds), *Go Into the Streets!*, Mahwah, NJ: Paulist Press, 2016, 109–24.

Rush, Ormond, 'Inverting the Pyramid: The *Sensus Fidelium* in a Synodal Church', *Theological Studies*, 78, June 2017, 299–325.

___ 'The Prophetic Office in the Church', in Richard R. Gaillardetz (ed.), *When the Magisterium Intervenes*, Collegeville, MN: Liturgical Press, 2012, 89–112.

Toner, Jules, 'A Method for Communal Discernment of God's Will', St Louis, MO: *Studies in the Spirituality of Jesuits*, vol. iii, n. 4, September 1971.

Twomey, Vincent D., 'The Second Vatican Council: An Irish Perspective', *Studies,* 101, winter 2012, 407–22.

___ 'The End of Irish Catholicism? Fifteen Years On', *Studies*, 106, spring 2017, 39–48.

Books/articles by Gerry O'Hanlon, which form the background to this book

Books

Theology in the Irish Public Square, Dublin: Columba Press, 2010.

A New Vision for the Catholic Church: A View from Ireland, Dublin: Columba Press, 2011.

A Dialogue of Hope (ed.) (with contributors David Begg, Michael Cronin, Iseult Honohan, Dermot A. Lane, Dermot McCarthy, Fergus O'Ferrall), Dublin: Messenger Publications, 2017.

Articles

'The Murphy Report – a response', *The Furrow*, 61, February 2010, 82–91.

'The future of the Catholic Church – a view from Ireland', *Studies*, 99, autumn 2010, 289–301.

'Culture and the Crisis in the Church', *The Furrow*, 61, December 2012, 655–66.

'The People of God: Towards a Renewed Church?', in Suzanne Mulligan (ed.), *Reaping the Harvest: Fifty Years after Vatican II*, Dublin: Columba Press, 2012.

'Towards an Assembly', *The Furrow*, 63, April 2012, 235–39.

'Irish Catholicism at a Crossroads', *Studies*, 101, winter 2012, 375–86.

'Razing the Ramparts – A Theological Reflection on Papal Primacy', *Doctrine and Life*, 62, July–August 2012, 35–52.

'The Pope's Interview: A Reflection', *Studies*, 102, autumn 2013, 279–82.

'Religious Freedom', *The Furrow,* 64, February 2013, 67–77.

'Whispers of the Spirit – the Church of the Future', *The Furrow*, 64, June 2013, 332–41.

'Learning from the Murphy Report: A Theological Reflection', *Studies*, 102, winter 2013, 423–33.

'On Consulting the Faithful – the Synod on the Family', *The Furrow*, 64, December 2013, 658–62.

'Re-Building Trust: The Role of the Catholic Church in Ireland', in Patrick Claffey, Joe Egan and Marie Keenan (eds), *Broken Faith, Why Hope Matters*, Bern: Peter Lang, 2013, 259–76.

'Voices of Hope: Echoes of the Divine', *Doctrine and Life*, 64, January 2014, 38–52.

'A Dream Fulfilled?', *The Furrow*, 65, March 2014, 169–78.

'Contested Legacies', *The Furrow*, 65, July–August 2014, 351–9.

'Where to Now? – Reflections on an Extraordinary Synod', *The Furrow*, 65, December 2014, 583–91.

'The Reform of the Church in her Missionary Outreach', in Enda McDonagh (ed.), *Performing

the Word, Festchrift for Ronan Drury, Dublin: Columba Press, 2014, 81–86.
'Deux ans après: des changements dans l'Église catholique, *En Question,* 112, mars 2015, 12–15.
'The Limerick Synod', *The Furrow,* 66, June 2015, 320–9.
'Discernment and the Synod on the Family', *Doctrine and Life,* 65, September 2015, 9–20.
'The Synod in Context', *Studies,* 104, autumn 2015, 251–60.
'The Quiet Revolution – Reflections on Synod 2015', *The Furrow,* 66, December 2015, 632–41.
'Vatican II as a Resource for the Renewal of the Church in Ireland for the Twenty-First Century',
   in Dermot A. Lane (ed.), *Vatican II in Ireland, Fifty Years On,* Bern: Peter Lang, 2015, 219–36.
'Church, Women, Authority – Why Not?', *Doctrine and Life,* 66, January 2016, 23–32.
'The Joy of Love – *Amoris Laetitia*', *The Furrow,* 67, June 2016, 328–36.
'Emerging Issues in Catholic Church Reform', *Doctrine and Life,* 66, July–August 2016, 3–15.
'Free Speech in the Church', *Studies,* 105, summer 2016, 199–211.
'The Catholic Church in Ireland Today', *Studies,* 106, spring 2017, 9–20 (originally published in
   Italian as 'La cattolicesimo in Irlanda è entrato in crisi?' in *La Civiltà Cattolica,* nr 3998, 14/28
   gennaio 2017, 161–74).
'Submission to the Australian Royal Commission into Institutional Responses to Child Sexual
   Abuse', *Doctrine and Life,* 67, March 2017, 53–64.
'Ireland and the Quiet Revolution in the Catholic Church', *The Furrow,* 68, May 2017, 259–67.

ACKNOWLEDGEMENTS

My thanks are due in the first instance to all those who read previous drafts of this book, and, in particular, to Donal Neary SJ for his encouragement and wise editorial advice. I am greatly indebted to Donal's staff at Messenger Publications for their professionalism and their readiness to publish so promptly.

I am grateful also to my Jesuit Provincial Leonard Moloney, and his successors Tom Layden and John Dardis, for their support, not least in freeing me up to enable the writing; to colleagues at the Jesuit Centre for Faith and Justice and Jesuit Communications, as well as colleagues in the theological and faith community in Ireland, from all churches; to my family Eileen and Randal, Frank and Freddy (and their families – Kieran, Cate, Lucy and Chloe; Rory, Karen, Erin, Alby and Saorise) and friends, in particular Fiona Fullam, Brian Lennon, Bill Toner and Jim Corkery for their unfailing encouragement, support and challenge. I want to say a particular word of thanks to all the parishes the length and breadth of Ireland who have invited me to share reflections and conversations with them over the last ten years or so – I can only hope that this book may be of some help to you in the difficult but exciting challenges that you, and we all, face.